C.E.O.: College is Extremely Overrated

Michael Hamlett, Jr.

DEDICATION

To my Lord and Savior, Jesus Christ, without you nothing is possible.

To my loving wife, Tiarra. Without you, I would have never tried
to pursue the impossible. Thank you for believing in me,
even when I didn't believe in myself.
I love you.

CONTENTS

DISCLAIMER

"Here's to the crazy ones, the misfits, the rebels, the troublemakers, the round pegs in the square holes... the ones who see things differently -- they're not fond of rules... You can quote them, disagree with them, glorify or vilify them, but the only thing you can't do is ignore them because they change things... they push the human race forward, and while some may see them as the crazy ones, we see genius, because the ones who are crazy enough to think that they can change the world, are the ones who do."- Steve Jobs

This book is not for everyone. Some of the content in it may offend you. Some may put it down, maybe even discard it or delete it from your reading device. The premise may even seem ridiculous or absurd to some. But this book is not for those people. This book is for the people that dare to be different. This is for the people that are tired of the status quo and want to take responsibility for their lives. This is for the people that ask questions, take risks, and solve problems. This book is for those who are bold enough to pursue passion and find their purpose. This book is for entrepreneurs.

1
INTRODUCTION

The college education system is the oldest institution in America. It's ingrained in American culture. Having a college degree is a sign of prosperity; it means you've "made it." It's a huge part of the American Dream. The college degree is also one of the most marketed ideas in America. Immigrants come to this country in hopes of having a better life for their kids. Parents aspire to have their kids obtain a college degree, even if they've never had one. Strangers can be proud of a recent college graduate simply because they've achieved this milestone. The College Degree is exalted to a god-like status. Any opinion raised against the college education system, including dropping out, is un-American.

Dropping out of college was the best decision I've ever made. It forced me to be creative and adjust to what most people avoid their whole lives: reality. Would I recommend that everyone drop out of college? Of course not! I also wouldn't recommend that everyone go to college either. It is an idea that has been force fed to many people from the time they are born until they begin taking their SATs. So why was dropping out of college the best decision I made? Because I learned a secret many people either never learn or have to learn the hard way. The secret is: in order to be successful in the real world, you need to do what most people avoid doing. You need to think. Like many teenagers, I had some problems. I had no money, worked a job that I hated, and realized college was not going to answer those issues, especially since paying tuition was one of my problems. After days of brainstorming, I decided to pursue a dream I've always had. I wanted to start my own business.

Now this is not a fairy tale filled with giggles and unicorns; this isn't an autobiography of how I did *it*, or a get-rich-quick-scheme-if you-follow-my-simple-steps, or an unraveling of a secret only revealed to me. I'll be the first to tell you that I don't have all of the answers; my life is messy and life is a process I'm still figuring out. Using my experiences, your experiences, and any other people's experiences, I want you to seriously consider all the real world consequences of the decisions you are going to make concerning college and business.

There's been an age-old debate of whether entrepreneurs should attend college or dive straight into their business. I'm personally for the latter. When I started my company, Don't Feed The Animals, I knew two things: I had no prior business experience and I knew I wanted to create a clothing brand. To create DFTA I knew I had to do everything in my power to learn and acquire the necessary skills to create, run, and operate a business. It didn't happen overnight, and I've made countless mistakes that taught me many lessons. But one thing was certain, and that was that college played a **minor** role in my real world business education. I didn't need college, and if you're serious enough about your business, have confidence, and are willing to put in all the work necessary to create a successful business, you probably don't need college either.

And if you don't know, now you know

Let's get one thing clear. Education is the key to advancing and becoming prosperous in any society. Proper education and understanding lead to knowledge and wisdom. We all know that knowledge is power. Without knowledge, and the prudence to use the knowledge gained through education, a person is rendered powerless, and the only decision to be made is to conform to the status quo – being complacent with society's standards. The status quo is never fun; no one wants to be mediocre. As an entrepreneur, the status quo should never be an option. Improvements can always be made and that should fuel an entrepreneur's mindset. An entrepreneur does not only take things at face value, but constantly questions everything. Entrepreneurs frequently ask "why?"

Ask yourself, "Why should I go to college? Do I need it? Is starting my business right now the best option for me? Should I wait?" Don't be afraid to ask tough questions. There is no such thing as a bad or dumb question, because asking a question signifies that many thinking processes are taking place. We'll get to those types of thinking processes later. Now you may be asking "Don't you receive an education in college?" and believe me when I say that it pains me to tell you that you are wrong. Sadly, people have created the misconception that college is the only way to become educated. They have even nicknamed it "higher education" as if this is the pinnacle of learning. There are many other cost effective, flexible, and convenient ways to learn what you need in order to start and operate your own business, without having a college degree.

Another misconception is that a person with a college degree is more likely to be a successful member of society compared with a person who did not attend college or (gasp!) dropped out. This is where the (dead) mantra "go to college, get good grades, get a job/career with nice benefits and a pension plan" stems from. Let's stop beating a dead horse. It's heartbreaking to hear people preach this mantra with such conviction as if it is a guaranteed formula. It's also quite annoying. This advice may have been true for the Baby Boomers and even Generation X, to a limited extent. But millennials are the "Facebook Generation." What many people fail to realize is that the world is always evolving, and the "guarantees" of yesterday are worthless today.

2
FOR WHAT IT'S WORTH

Before we continue, let's look at the history of college, its intended purpose, and the economic implications of what it has become today.

The structure of the college curriculum, as well as the structure for the United States' education system, is modeled after the ancient Egyptian and Greek's views on holism. As holistic thinkers, the Egyptians and Greeks believed in viewing the world and its interconnectedness as a whole. They believed that education should follow this same approach, teaching varied material at once, to display the interwoven tapestry of the world we live in. It's a beautiful concept, but I'll explain why I don't agree with their approach later.

Fast forward to the late eleventh century when the first universities were formed. The oldest universities include the University of Bologna and the University of Oxford. Before the University of Bologna began teaching law and other subjects, ecclesiastic schools were training priests. These ecclesiastic schools were dedicated to training individuals who were called by God to be ministers and clergy within the Church. They knew their purpose (to instruct people in the Christian faith) and sought training to do so. The University of Bologna was the first school to begin training individuals for other professions, such as politics, law and medicine. The oldest English university, Oxford, has the motto "Dominus Illuminatio Mea" meaning "The Lord is my Light." Why is this important? I think it's important to point out the ironic relationship higher education has with Christianity.

The concept of the university was born out of the need to train people for their calling, particularly those who desired to be priests. In our post-post modern world, Christianity and education (or reason) seem to be in opposition. In fact, if it weren't for Christian thinkers and leaders, the current scholarly skeptics wouldn't have halls and classrooms to challenge Christian ideology. But I digress. Let's get back to the history of college, its Christian roots, and what it is today.

When the Puritans left Europe, they this idea of creating institutions as training centers for church leaders. The Puritans must have found it vital to establish Harvard College, given that the Puritans settled in New England in 1620 (Plymouth Colony) and the Massachusetts Bay Colony was established in 1629. It's amazing to think that Harvard, America's oldest college, was founded in 1636 and chartered in 1650. Within seven years of creating the Massachusetts Bay Colony, the Puritans concluded that it was essential for ministers to be trained on how they should shepherd God's people. Plaques in Harvard still tell the story of how the Puritans came to America, established the college to train ministers and how clergyman John Harvard donated half of his estate in order to ensure the college would continue to be a *seminary* that advances learning. John Harvard wouldn't recognize the Harvard College we have today.

Similar to the progression of higher education in Europe, law, politics and medicine were added as fields of study. College was people centered, rather than career oriented. Individuals went to college to pursue people. As I mentioned before, ministers went to college to spiritually care for people. Others studied medicine to physically care for people. Lawyers and politicians studied in order to lead and govern people well. In essence, colleges and university were created in order to train leaders as they follow their purpose and passion. These leaders weren't simply looking for a resume boost; they were looking to use their gifts and talents to have a lasting influence on the world around them.

William and Mary College is similar to Harvard in its founding purpose. Law and medicine were added to the college curriculum after their seminary schools were established. The original purpose of college began to change when the American

Revolutionary War and the Age of Reason swept through America. In 1779, Thomas Jefferson led the charge in reorganizing William and Mary by abolishing the grammar and divinity school. He did this in order to give the university a "more general diffusion of knowledge." Thomas Jefferson repurposed the idea of college from an institution specialized in helping individuals find their calling, into a secularized institution modeled after classical Greek philosophy. I guess the reasoning was to look backward (to the Greeks' holistic approach) in order to progress forward. Welcome to the *new* and *improved* University.

3
THE ECONOMICS OF COLLEGE

I started writing this book in 2010. I'll admit, I was extremely frustrated with my college experience and it was evident in the first edition of this book. This made me a little reluctant to promote the book. In fact, I noticed that if I did share my opinion about the institution of college, I'd be met with serious opposition. College grads, parents, and most high school aged young adults simply don't want to hear a college dropout talk about college in a negative way. I get it. But we seriously have to ask ourselves a couple of questions. The first is: are we failing to see college as a big business that is disinterested in the future of its students (customers)? Next, why is our obsession with this institution at a level where we can't have a healthy discussion about the pros, and more importantly the cons, of trying to obtain a college degree?

Let's briefly tackle the first question. Collegiate athletes are very aware of the fact that colleges are big businesses only concerned with its well-being. Talking about student athletes, work-study programs, and NCAA sanctions is beyond the scope of this book. But you can do your due diligence by watching an ESPN documentary or by Googling "NCAA Antitrust." What about those students who aren't athletes? Also, why would an entrepreneur be against a business?

To answer the second question, I'd much rather call a spade a spade. A lot of people have viewed college as institutions that were created primarily for public benefit. Unfortunately, that isn't the case at this point in American history. So if we are honest about college being a big business with big profits, let's address the next question: what's our obsession with the College Degree?

As I stated in the last chapter, our educational system takes a holistic approach to education. This type of education disregards an individual's passions and gifting, curtails creativity, and causes people to lose focus on their purpose in life. We lie to children when we tell them that they can be whatever they want to be. We do that in a couple of ways.

If a person has little aptitude for science it would be almost impossible for them to become a physicist. We should be telling kids to find their purpose, rather than aimlessly pursuing careers they weren't designed to do. If everything happens for a reason, then everyone is designed for a specific purpose. Teaching kids to study information that is not essential to real life issues, and that's not in line with their purpose, will only frustrate them.

Children can't be whatever they want to be. It's idealistic and sounds nice, but it's not true. Children need to follow the curriculum standard. If they can't pass a subject like math, even though they may show a high level of intelligence in another subject, they could be at risk of failing. Failing a class would hinder them from growing in their stronger subject. In the context of college, if you can't pass your "general education requirements" (what I like to call "second high school"), you won't be able to graduate. Which is actually the whole point of going to college: to study something you would enjoy because you feel called to pursue that specific passion. Kids can't be whatever they want to be because we are too busy telling them to be good at everything, rather than teaching them to be excellent in whatever they were created to do.

College isn't the place to "find yourself." It's too expensive for that. Since 1979, the cost of a college education has risen 1190%. If you still think college is really dedicated to your development as an individual, stop paying tuition for a semester and see what the consequences are. In almost all other business structures, customers have an influence on the direction of a company. If a pizza store sells slices at a 100% premium, customers can buy from another store, and that causes the first pizza store to bring their prices down. A smart pizza storeowner would listen to customer feedback, bring prices down, and even offer new kinds of pizza slices for their customers to enjoy. A successful pizza owner will work hard to attract new customers and keep them as happy as possible. Also, a pizza storeowner knows that everyone isn't a "pizza person." Some people like burgers, and that's O.K. When it comes to the college institution, we don't see these types of interactions. Colleges seem to defy economic and market forces.

"I have never let my schooling interfere with my education."
- Mark Twain

Colleges are only concerned with protecting their prestige, paying their staff, and attracting new students (clients). Those who perform well in a school setting (i.e. test taking, memorizing information, and sitting through lectures) are recruited to a university since they have demonstrated that they are most likely to continue performing at a high level of "schooling." This protects the prestige of the college. Colleges also hire well-schooled professors, further adding and protecting their prestige. In order to pay these professors, colleges need to charge tuition (fees). For the privilege of being taught by intelligent professors, students pay top dollar. Most of the time, these are dollars they don't have, so they borrow. Because the U.S. federal government subsidizes loans, colleges know that they can increase their tuition rates. Students pay the colleges what they can, and the government covers the rest of the tuition costs. Colleges aren't concerned with their student's ability to repay debt or the increase in tuition. Colleges (both private nonprofit and public) aren't doing background checks to make sure their students can pay tuition rates that increase at an inflation adjusted average of 3.51% per year! They are not serving their students well. Unfortunately, the concept of having a college degree has been embedded into our society so deeply that most of the population sees the College Degree as the main response to socio-economic issues. Colleges don't have to work as hard as other businesses, but receive all of the benefits.

The current trend for those pursuing a college degree isn't to pursue what we were made to do, but to pursue a better quality of life. If we are going to college for the sole purpose of having a better quality of life, we are disregarding our dreams, our passions and our purpose. We sacrifice our time, energy, and money for a better life. Tim Keller, a pastor in NYC, brilliantly stated, "if you want to locate your idol, think of what you're most afraid of." We worship and protect the things that matter most to us. As I stated earlier, the College Degree has been exalted to god-like status. I think for many college graduates, if they are told that college is overrated or overvalued, they get defensive because there's truth to the statement. They may have sacrificed their dreams and time and are afraid they won't be compensated for it. Unfortunately, in America our god is Money, the priest is College and our greatest fear is that neither will validate nor fulfill us.

Before I talk about America's unhealthy infatuation with the college degree, I want to discuss three things. First, what happens when everyone has a degree? Next, when did our economy begin to emphasize the need for a college degree? Finally, what are the current and future economic implications?

Supply and Supply

Everyone knows the basic principle of economics: supply and demand. When supply is high, demand is low and prices fall. When supply is low, demand is high and prices rise. This principle applies to every market – even the job market. When skills are emphasized in a job description, applicants need to evaluate whether they have these skills before they apply. When they apply, HR managers scan through resumes looking for particular skills to ensure they are not wasting time interviewing candidates that will not be a good fit for the company. The need (demand) for great employees meeting a required skill set, is fulfilled by the candidate (supply) with those qualifications. The job market is efficient and everyone is relatively happy. As the company adapts to market changes in supply and demand, employees need to adapt, otherwise they'll lose their job. For new applicants, they need to continue to sharpen their skills and demonstrate them to their potential employer. The person with the best skills gets the job, and the company improves because they are more efficient in finding the right talent.

When a college degree is the standard for meaningful employment, things change dramatically. Credentials become more valuable than skills. Applicants that aren't skilled for positions may apply simply because they've met the degree requirements. Those who have the skills but lack the credentials of a college degree aren't considered for an interview; the company interviews candidates that may not be suitable for the job. Newly hired employees could become frustrated because they lack applicable skills, or lack passion for the role they have. The company might perform at a lower rate of productivity, given they haven't found the right person for the position they are trying to fill. This – mismatching candidates to positions based on credentials and not experience – seems to be the hiring trend for HR managers, and even applies to entry-level positions.

Double Bubble, Toil and Trouble

Now, what happens when a college degree is required for an entry-level position, and skills aren't emphasized as much as they should be? Jobseekers begin to believe that advanced degrees will lead to a better probability of landing the job. Their logic simply follows the hiring trend. If I'm a jobseeker and everyone has a high school diploma, while I have a bachelor's degree, I've differentiated myself. I have an easier time marketing myself as a better candidate. If everyone has a bachelor's, I'll need a master's degree. If everyone now gets a master's, I'll simply get another master's degree or even make the commitment for a PhD. Unfortunately, the answer to better employment isn't continuing college education, it's an emphasis on skills and passion.

We are currently in the Education Bubble. Nobel Laureate Robert Shiller's defines a bubble as "a situation in which excessive public expectations of future price increases cause prices to be temporarily elevated." The Education Bubble directly affects the Job Market. The current public expectation is that higher education means a higher income. As we move up the educational ladder with advanced degrees, we expect our salaries to increase as well. The future price increase should be our future salary. As people continue to place their future career expectations on obtaining a college degree, they inadvertently increase the price of a college education.

Similar to the Tech Bubble in the late '90s and early 2000s, as well as the Housing Bubble in 2007, the Education Bubble's price for a college degree continues to rise while its value is stagnant. If the value of a degree is found in its ability to help graduates find meaningful employment, then the degree (in relation to what people are willing to sacrifice for it) is overvalued. In other financial bubbles, the link between price and value was broken until the bubble finally burst. To clarify, the title of my book isn't "College is Extremely UNNECESSARY", it's "College is Extremely OVERRATED." Students are paying exorbitant prices for education, with little to show for it. The college degree, the college experience, and the initial purpose of college are not worthless; they're just overvalued.

In 2010 a bachelor's degree served as semi-adequate resume differentiation. The 2015 job market, however, is saturated with job listings requiring advanced degrees for entry-level positions. The number of people with bachelor's degrees has risen and increased the supply of this type of job candidate. Company's are now no longer in the market for graduates unless they have, or are pursuing, a master's degree. In 2020, will PhDs be necessary for entry-level positions? Graduates are starting to realize that a college degree isn't as valuable as it once was. Almost everyone has one, and employers aren't willing to pay top dollar for it anymore.

The job market is now a market of supply and supply. Employers have so many applicants to choose from that it gets difficult to ensure they are choosing the best one for their position. The U.S. economy wasn't always this way, so what changed?

The Big Business of Federal Student Loans

One of the first rules of economics is that people respond to incentives. What incentives caused Americans to flock towards collegiate institutions? The first incentive was affordability. With the National Defense Education Act of 1958, President Eisenhower made it possible for the Federal government to grant scholarships and offer loans to individuals pursuing a college degree in mathematics, engineering, and teaching. The goal of this act was to help the U.S. stay educationally ahead of the former USSR during the Cold War. The act also encouraged schools to strengthen their math, science and foreign language programs throughout all grade levels (which also explains our current emphasis on these particular subjects). In 1965, President Johnson's Great Society and The Higher Education Act gave education loans to those who were in economic need. The increased accessibility and affordability of a college degree caused a huge rise in college enrollment between the 1960's and 70s.

Of course, the government responds to incentives as well. In 1972, President Nixon's administration and Congress created the government-sponsored entity we've all come to lovingly know as Sallie Mae. The Student Loan **Marketing** Association was created to ensure that banks lend to students, and even bought back student loans. Today, Sallie Mae is privatized but the federal government is still an active player in the student loan business. According to the U.S. Treasury Department's monthly statements, in April 2015 the U.S. Government held over $954 million of student loan debt. To put that in perspective, of the **$1.2 trillion of student loan debt**, the federal government owns and profits from 84% of it. Read more on taxes in chapter 10 to see why the government continues to encourage college enrollment.

Funky Times

The 1960s-70s was an interesting time in U.S. history. Two of the factors contributing to the rise in college attendance were the Vietnam War deferments and government subsidies in the form of student loans. I'm not going to get into a political treatise, so I'll just give an overview of this era and the economic implications for us today. As more men enrolled in colleges, the idea of college became synonymous with a better life (by avoiding the draft). During this time period, Federal Reserve Chairman Paul Volcker boldly allowed interest rates to rise in order to combat inflation. The downside to this risky and unpopular decision was high unemployment. As businesses downsized, college became an attractive alternative to simply waiting for the economy to recover. According to the National Center for Education Statistics, college enrollment nearly tripled from 4.1 million in 1961 to over 11.5 million in 1979. By 1983, as inflation dipped to a manageable 3.2%, the U.S. economy began to boom and businesses were once again willing to hire. Those who attended four-year institutions in 1979 would have been graduating around this time. The U.S. stock market would enter into one of the greatest bull markets in history, and the '80s would be marked by wealth and excess. This was the absolute best time to be a college graduate, as firms were willing and able to pay top dollar for job seekers. The economy was able to not only absorb the supply of college graduates, but also compensated them generously.

A college degree was not only a means to a better financial life but a status symbol, just as iconic as a gold watch. However, the increase in the standard of living for the American worker was a buy-product of the economy's bounce back form the inflation ridden '70s. It wasn't *primarily* a result of an increase in the amount of college graduates, but in large part a result of the economic cycle.

4
INCOME GENERATION

From the time we begin working our goal is to save up enough money so that we don't have to work later in life. Essentially, we work in order to retire. Our hope is to be able to travel, take leisure time, and do what we want to do. We want to buy back the time we spent working. Our goal then is to increase our income, so that we can live off of our wealth accumulation. We use our time to work in order to get more money. However, I think it's better to have our money work to buy us time.

Before I explain further, I need to concede a fact about the income gap between a person with a high school diploma and a person with either an associates or a bachelor's degree. Between years 18 – 36, a person with a high school diploma generates *more income* than a person with either an associate's degree or a bachelor's degree. After that, those with a degree generate more income than those with a high school education. I'll explain why a higher income isn't necessarily the answer to your financial struggles in the following paragraphs and in chapter 10. Here's a graph of this phenomena from the College Board report *Education Pays 2013*:

FIGURE 1.3
Estimated Cumulative Full-Time Earnings (in 2011 Dollars) Net of Loan Repayment for Tuition and Fees, by Education Level

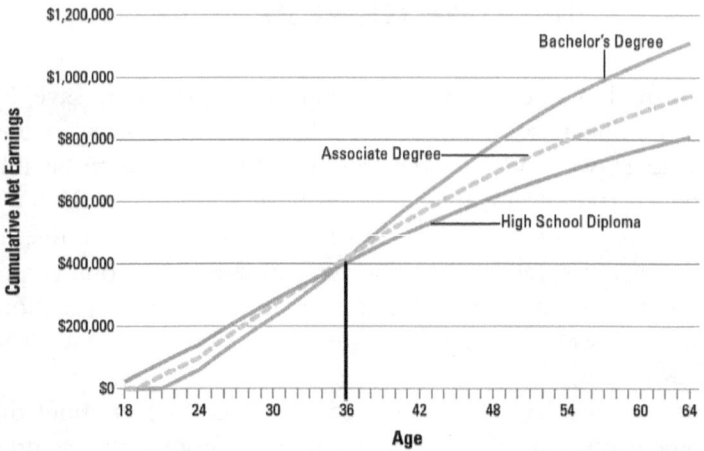

Now, you're probably thinking I'm crazy for more than one reason. If you didn't already think I was crazy for writing this book in the first place, you're probably thinking I'm crazy for referencing the College Board and for using one of their graphs (that would appear to contradict the purpose of this book). Two people can look at the same information and come to different conclusions, and so I hope you can (at the very least) consider the following.

Whether you have taken a course in finance or not, we all know the basic foundation of the **time value of money**: a dollar today is always worth more than a dollar tomorrow. This is primarily because of inflation, as well as risk and opportunity cost, but I want to focus on the fact that a dollar today is worth more than a dollar tomorrow. I want to also emphasize, that a dollar today is most definitely worth more than a dollar 18 years from now.

Let's identify some of the assumptions from the chart. The first assumption is that a college graduate will be employed immediately upon graduation. The next assumption is that each person is working full time at the median income for his or her education level. Finally, loan repayments have been deducted from graduate incomes for ten years at 6.8% interest. I think this graph is a phenomenal representation of a dollar for dollar comparison between each education level's earned incomes. Of course, taxes aren't accounted for, and neither are extra income sources, such as business or investment income, but that would make things a bit more complicated. Let's get back to the time value of money.

If we want our money to work for us, and help us get to retirement faster, we need to invest our money as quickly as we can. Let's assume you're a savvy high school graduate who decides to invest $100/month at a conservative 7% annual return (this is slightly less than the average 9% return of the stock market but also slightly higher than the average yield of corporate, municipal and treasury bonds). Over an 18-year period, the high school graduate would have accumulated $42,329.81! Not to be outdone, the BA graduate also invests the same amount at the same rate of return once they begin working.

Break-even age (36) – Average age at BA graduation (22) = 14. Over a 14-year period, the college graduate accumulates $28,076.03, a difference of over $14,000 in favor of the high school graduate. Since our primary concern is retirement, let's stretch the example to the conventional retirement age of 65. Our high school graduate would have accumulated, a whopping $409,894.14! The BA graduate accumulates $308,489.10, which is obviously nothing to scoff at, but a 4-year difference results in a $100,000 difference over the course of a lifetime.

Investing as early as you can isn't the only way to achieve financial freedom; saving more of your income will get you there faster than you thought. Saving makes investment possible. It's also something you can do at any income or education level.

If you haven't heard, the concept of early retirement is at the forefront of financial conversations. It's beyond the scope of this book to get into the details and nuances but I want to make a point about saving more and investing earlier. If you visit networthify.com you can crunch the numbers on their early retirement calculator. Let's say you saved 25% of your income and invested it at 7% with a 4% withdrawal rate (the amount you withdraw from your investments), it would take just 27.1 years to retire. That's age 45 for a disciplined high school graduate. Let's say you're incredibly disciplined and are able to save 50% of your income, it would only take 15 years to retire. Imagine being a high school graduate that's retired at age 33!

I know saving 50% of your income can be extremely difficult. I just want to demonstrate that higher income isn't necessarily the answer to your money woes. I also wanted to show how saving and investing a nominal amount like $100 over a lifetime can generate a huge return. If you aren't saving or investing now, I hope this chapter convinces you to start NOW! I also hope that you would give some sound advice to a high school graduate near you; 4 years is a precious amount of time and $100,000 is an amount they can't afford to lose.

5
NO MONEY BACK GUARANTEE

An Offer We Don't Refuse

Let's make a deal. Imagine I came to you with this business proposal: give me $100,000 and, in four years, you may see a return on your investment. You'll have to work long hours, and even all-nighters at certain points, but there is a possibility (not the guarantee) that you may be successful. This investment could be the "end all be all" quick fix to your current socio-economic problems. Would you take the deal? Or, would you look at me as if I'm a scam artist?

Unfortunately, it's an offer that colleges continue to make. It's an offer we can't refuse. We don't think twice about the implications of giving blind advice to our youth. We don't ask enough questions to see what their interests are and how they can pursue their passions. We simply tell them to go to college. Now, I do believe that business is a better alternative (read chapter 6), but I also don't think everyone is an entrepreneur. In the same way we wouldn't advise a person to simply start a business without doing research beforehand, we also shouldn't suggest that every young person attend college. My example shows that we intuitively know a bad business deal when we see one. We are extremely cautious when we make investments or think about starting a business. We understand that there are risks involved, and many of us wouldn't start a business because of those risks. Why don't we take that same approach when it comes to the College Degree? We're too quick to suggest higher education as the best investment that young people can make in themselves. We're setting them up for a bad deal.

According to the College Board the average per year cost of tuition was $31,231 at private colleges, $9,139 for state residents at public colleges, and $22,958 for out of state residents attending public universities in 2014-2015. These costs represent a 3.3% average rise from the 2013-2014 school year. The tuition average is $21,109 per year, *not including* room and board, books, and other miscellaneous college expenses like food and transportation. The average starting salary for a college graduate in 2015 was $45,327 in gross pay. After the 25% tax rate, college graduates take home $33,995 in net pay. When we deduct frivolous expenses like housing and food, using MIT's study on the national cost of living, college graduates have a whopping $19,415 annually, or $1,617/month at their disposal. We expect college graduates to have a full grasp of personal finance, even though most aren't taught that in school, as they use this surplus to navigate the real world. I'd also like to note that I used Ohio's living expenses, since it was closest to the national average. When we use the numbers from major cities like NYC, where many millennials flock to, the net income is staggeringly low.

Can an economy that creates financially crippled young adults continue to sustain itself? It's already a financial tragedy that our youth aren't able to find meaningful employment (or work that engages their innate abilities); we're also enslaving them to a burden of debt they most likely won't pay off until they're middle-aged. We're cutting the future American workforce at the knees and making it increasingly difficult to have a moderate quality of life. College education is the most expensive it's ever been. College graduates are the most indebted they've ever been. For many, the American dream is just a fantasy, while their present circumstance is a nightmare. A society filled with overworked and underpaid employees is a terrible one. A society filled with overeducated and undercapitalized workers is a tragedy.

Socio-Economic Cure-all?

If a teenager comes to you for advice about work and direction, what would you suggest? If a 20something were frustrated with their current career path, what advice would be given? What does a 40something do in order to beef up their resume and get the promotion? When a 7 year old is asked the most unhelpful question, "What do you want to be when you grow up?" don't we steer them away from their creative dreams, careers we deem are not going to make money? In all of these occasions, we're most likely to answer, or have been given the response, to go back to school. Sometimes, pursuing a degree program is prescribed before any probing questions are asked. The prescription of the college degree and our society's diagnosis for every socio-economic ailment is more alarming than the school nurse who gives ice packs to every sick child.

Teen crime rates are rising? They should be in college. The male workforce is shrinking? They should learn new skills in college. Single mothers are struggling to provide for their family? I know a college that can give you financial aid. We're forgetting that everyone is different, with a dynamic struggle that can't be fixed with the same solution. Quite frankly, we aren't asking enough questions about people as individuals, because it's much easier to give a quick solution and walk away. It's a completely different thing to be relationally invested in an individual, and treat them as the distinct person they are. We need to direct people towards their passions, instead of a degree program.

The one guarantee you have when leaving college, whether or not you graduate, is debt. I know that this was a major problem for me, and I didn't even graduate! Many would argue that taking on student loans are an investment in yourself and that the salary you'll be making after you graduate should compensate for it. First of all, it's not advisable to put yourself in a financial hole without having a plan to get yourself out of that hole. You'll end up being buried alive in debt, literally, and you'll kiss your dreams of home ownership goodbye if you can't make student loan payments. Why set yourself up for failure? Next, this reasoning is based on two key variables; the first is that you actually graduate and the next one is that you actually find a job after you graduate. The one thing you can bank on after attending college (whether you graduate or not) is a mountain of debt. Also, if you select a competitive career path – one with many applicants with a small number of available jobs – or if your major generally does not lead to a high-paying job it will be difficult to pay back those student loans. It is irrational to get into debt for a job you can only hope to find.

You *could* justify student loan debt *if* you paid everything in full and never swiped your credit card to make a purchase. Oh wait! How could I possibly forget the "Class of (enter year here)" tees/hoodies and the wonderful "Proud parent of (enter school name her) graduate" bumper stickers? And let's not forget that they do give you a nice piece of paper that you can frame, stating that you have indeed graduated. Unfortunately, you can't trade these in for any real cash value to pay off those student loans you've accumulated. When I first started writing this book, the median household income in America was about $44,000 in 2010. In 2010, the average student loan debt was about $25,000 for those that graduated. That's more than 50% of debt to the average income for one year!

In 2015, the average student loan debt has ballooned to $35,051 (the most ever for college graduates) while the median household income has increased to $51,939. In the five-year period from 2010-2015 median household income has increased by just under $8,000 while student loan debt has increased by just over $10,000. Considering that wages do not rise nearly as fast as tuition increases, the spread between income and student loan debt will only get worse in America.

Be certain of this: college does not guarantee that employers will sabotage each other to hire you at your graduation. The fact remains that on paper, resume paper to be specific, you may have the same credentials as thousands of other applicants. Even if you graduated from one of the top schools in the country, if the economy is down and no one is hiring, you better start thinking of more creative ways to beef up your resume, or start a business.

College also fails to guarantee that you will find a job relevant to your major. I'm sure you can name five people whom have a job that has nothing to do with what they studied in college. I can name at least ten. Now, if you are somehow able to pay off all your student loans, graduate with little to no debt, receive employment relevant to your major, all within the six-month post graduate grace period then you'd be an anomaly.

Here's the kicker: even if you are able to get hired in a reasonable amount of time, let's say 6 months, after you graduate, there is absolutely no such thing as "job security." It is a myth preached by those who embrace The Mantra. If a company is downsized, or even worse, if the company goes out of business, no one's job is safe. This is a fact. It doesn't matter if you were the vice president of an important department with a fancy name; you will be pounding the pavement sending out resumes if the company you work for isn't generating profits.

Unfortunately, I also know people who have been downsized, and I'm sure you do as well. As an entrepreneur, you must not become trapped into thinking that college is the only path to education, you cannot believe in job security, and you need to stop spreading The Mantra to others. "Go to college and get an education" isn't very open-minded. This mantra gives you a simple formula: College = Success. However, I dare you to Google "Successful Entrepreneurs Without a College Degree." I want you to see with your own eyes all the lists that have been compiled. There are many entrepreneurs you've never even heard of that make these lists, and even more that don't!

I've included a small list of very successful entrepreneurs who never attended college, for your convenience, at the end of this book. Money isn't the ultimate indicator of success, but as an economist, it's interesting to see how well people have done financially with the choices they've made. I'd also ask you to take note of how many people on just one particular list that are at least a millionaire. I'm sure you'll be surprised at the number of billionaires you'll find.

Overrated and Overvalued

What's wrong with college? Well college has done a poor job of equipping students to face the real world. There are basic skills every person should have and college fails to teach these skills to the students they serve. College fails to give people a financial education. We will talk more about financial education shortly, but know that without a solid financial education, you're essentially running on quicksand. It's frustrating to count the number of adults I know that can't explain what a balance sheet, income statement, or cash flow statement are. Many don't even understand that they are all different. A balance sheet is the snapshot of a company's (or person's) assets, liabilities and equity (or net worth for individuals). An income statement records the revenue, expenses and net profit of a company. The cash flow statement tracks the cash that comes into and goes out of the business. Many people haven't been taught the importance of a budget and keeping one. Because of this, their spending habits are out of control. The bottom line is: **college teaches students to become employees.** There's nothing wrong if you want to be an employee, employees are essential cogs to businesses, but if you're a true entrepreneur then college is not the place for you.

The purpose of college is to teach you skills exclusive to a certain field with the expectation that you'll find a job within that field to apply those skills. However, it does not teach you to think for yourself, but instead to follow orders. It does not teach you to become a real problem solver, but to plug the numbers until things work - to be a bean counter. College also fails to give you real hands on experience in your field (and I'm not talking about internships). In the actual structure of the curriculum for college courses, theory seems to be more important than practicality.

Instead let's ask this question: What does it truly take to become a professional at something? It takes approximately

10,000 hours to master a skill set at a professional level as stated by Malcolm Gladwell in *Outliers*. This does not in any way say that you need a college degree. It emphasizes experience. Experience trumps a college degree. Don't believe me? Imagine running your company, would you want to hire someone who has no idea what they're doing but was taught what to do, or would you rather hire someone who already knows what to do and has insight from their experience? I would choose the latter every time. Writing theoretical papers taught by a professor, who is likely not the originator of those theories, does not constitute experience. Experience requires action.

Like I said earlier, a professor teaching business theory is not the person you want to get business advice from – you'll want advice from a businessman. That's the equivalent to asking legal advice from your cousin who watches *Law and Order*. If you want to learn about business, read stories about entrepreneurs who have been there – started companies and failed – and then learned from their mistakes. A professor can only give you second hand information; a real entrepreneur can give you much more insight because of their experience.

Real world experience will always beat a high GPA. In fact, the further removed you are from school, the more irrelevant your GPA becomes. There is a major difference between knowing what to do and actually doing it. Knowledge is power, but without the wisdom or understanding to use and apply that knowledge in the most effective way possible, then knowledge is useless. Knowledge is necessary, wisdom is crucial, and wisdom comes from understanding. Understanding comes from experience, making mistakes and learning from them.

College, and the education system in general, prides itself on giving kids knowledge, but what about the application of that knowledge? It's about time we started looking for ways to apply the knowledge we gain, instead of filling our brains with random facts that get us nowhere. This is where college fails at preparing the workforce of tomorrow to face the real world.

I would much rather have a resume showing that I can

complete certain tasks than have a piece of paper that says I know how certain tasks should be done. For the cost of a college education, I'd expect a better return on my investment than a degree that doesn't even guarantee I'll find a job. In business, before an investment is made, the business owner has to make sure that the investment can pay for itself, so that the business doesn't lose money. As an entrepreneur, you shouldn't be in the business of losing money.

If you are looking to open up your own business, is the degree really worth the money? Let's use a couple of scenarios and see. You've just graduated high school (or are in high school) and have a business idea. You don't really know, however, if you want to go to college or start the business first. For an in-state public four-year college in 2011-12, the average cost was about $8,244 a year, excluding books and additional college costs, according to collegeboard.com. So if you go to a public in-state college, you will spend almost $10,000 on that college's core curriculum. This is not even on specific classes for your major or skill sets you can immediately apply to your business. Of course there is always financial aid, but we also aren't putting a value to the time spent in that first year versus time you could be spending on your business, so we'll stick with these figures. If instead of going to college, you spent this first year working a minimum wage job, part time for 24 hours a week, while simultaneously setting the foundation for your business endeavor, you will have made $9,048 before taxes and any other living expenses. That's almost a $20,000 spread between college costs and potential income, excluding any taxes, expenses, or financial aid of course.

Depending on how much effort you have put into starting your business, by the end of year one you should have laid at least the groundwork to get your business up and running. People may argue that you have nothing to fall back on, no backup plan, in case things go wrong. You'll need to have confidence in yourself and your business venture. This is not to say you should make unwise decisions just because you believe in everything you do. You should always take **calculated** risks. The point is that you shouldn't let the idea of failing dictate your decisions. It shows a lack of confidence. If you aren't confident enough in your abilities to learn how to develop, run, and manage your business, then entrepreneurship is probably not the best option for you. Since we live in the real world and usually fail before we succeed, let's say the business fails. What now? Well you've learned what didn't work for you. You can choose to improve on your weaknesses or abandon the business and do something else. Maybe starting a business from the ground up wasn't the best fit for you. Maybe buying a business is more in tune with your entrepreneurial goals. If things don't go according to plan it isn't the end of the world, and it doesn't make you a bad entrepreneur. You can always start again, with more experience, and give it your best effort.

6
PURSUING PASSION

The Road Less Traveled

So far, we've looked at how overrated the college degree is when it's touted as a socio-economic cure-all. In the following chapters, I'll explain why owning a business is a better alternative to pursuing a college degree (of course college graduates can own businesses as well). I'll also explain why I believe college isn't a necessary prerequisite for entrepreneurs and how a person who is ready to take the plunge into entrepreneurship can get into the entrepreneurial mindset. However, this chapter is meant to highlight a fundamental aspect of our human existence that we neglect when we give or take advice (whether to own a business or get a degree) without asking questions. We forget that everyone should aim to find their purpose by pursuing their passion.

When we tell people to go to college, or blame teachers for low performing students (especially in subjects like math and science) or when even when we tell people that "they can do anything they set their mind to," we disservice them by disregarding them as a person. Everyone has a unique calling and is gifted in particular ways. Everyone isn't meant to go to college, or start a business; but they should find their purpose. Everyone isn't going to be a physicist, and arithmetic can be off-putting for many, but we shouldn't try and tweak teaching methods in order to peak student's interest for any subject. Rather than study all subjects at one time (holism, the Greek and Egyptian teaching method) and penalize those who can't keep up, we should help students focus on their strengths. We should set healthy boundaries and be honest with ourselves and with each other. We can't do everything and anything we want, and we shouldn't strive to.

My point is that we can't continue to give general advice to individuals. We need be invested in the well being of the people we engage, rather than simply give well intentioned (but ultimately useless) advice.

I have friends that went to college in order to pursue their passion, and have been successful because the college degree wasn't the end of the road for them. It was a small step in a lifelong journey of purpose. I applaud them and anyone who chases after their dreams. We should always encourage people to use their abilities to find their purpose. I have a special place in my heart for the teachers that are truly called to teach (and a master's degree is usually required for this career path). I'm most definitely not opposed to the fact that many people have to get a degree in order to live out their calling in life. I'm just adamantly against the notion that college is *always* a necessary goal that we should encourage our kids and young people to attain. More often than not, it's a huge detour.

College can be a barrier to entry into the Job Market. It can be a barrier for people that want to pursue their dreams because they feel obligated to pursue a degree. Pressure from parents/family members to pursue a degree, even though it may not be beneficial to the individual, can also stifle their ability to find meaningful work. The college institution negates the individual. If we are made for a purpose, shouldn't we primarily pursue that purpose rather than a degree? We're not pursuing our purpose by simply attending college. We're just fulfilling requirements in a curriculum. Before we can study our interests, or our major, we need to muddle through required classes. We may ask ourselves, **"Why am I here?"** It's a question we should ask before we pursue a degree.

Why ask "why?" It informs us of our purpose. We need to find the purpose behind the things we do in order to ensure they align with our own purpose. We ask questions to find the answers we either don't know or have forgotten. Throughout our lives, we can lose the clarity of our purpose. Now, I believe that God isn't simply the greatest artist; he's also the greatest engineer. There's beauty in the perfect union between form and function. All of creation displays this union and we're enamored with it, because it reminds us of purpose. The beauty of a fulfilled purpose captivates us, because we long to find it.

When we see someone who has a lot of potential, we get frustrated. It's because we see a life that isn't living out its purpose. I think that this is one of the many reasons why the "college route" is suggested to every person.

Whether you're a child, a high school student, or going through a mid-life crisis, the roadmap of life is often an unclear one. Life is messy and we want a quick fix solution to our problems. Since our lives revolve around money as a means to get the things we want and need, we are fixated on whatever path can get us the most money (usually with the least amount of work) in the shortest amount of time, regardless of the fact that we aren't pursuing our passion.

College isn't a cure-all or the answer to our income gap. That's not the purpose of college. As I stated earlier, a major myth of the college degree is that it will set us apart. Unfortunately, we can't be set apart from other candidates if the basic requirement for an entry-level position is a B.A. All the candidates have one. Our passions usually fuel our strengths. We need to focus on our strengths rather than our weaknesses. A college education charges us to work on both, but that's not the most productive use of our time. It disregards what we are gifted in and born to do. It's also frustrating, knowing that we are simply not designed to pursue certain things, and if we can't pass a certain course, the degree is even more elusive. We need to evaluate our strengths and weaknesses, and work hard at utilizing our talents. This is not to say college is unnecessary. It serves a purpose and can be good. But it is grossly overvalued. College institutions seem to have a monopoly on validation, and we're willing to pay top dollar for it.

Free(lance) Is For Me

According to a 2014 study conducted by Edelman Berland, 53 million American workers are freelancers. This represents 34% of the U.S. workforce and is drastically different from the Baby Boomer and Gen X workforce demographic; 38% of Millennials are freelancing. What is causing this shift in the workforce? 68% of those surveyed said that extra income was the reason they pursued freelancing. While 42% said that flexibility in their schedule was the primary reason. Each group, though not mutually exclusive, is saying that they want more freedom. It is also interesting to not that 77% of those surveyed said that they made the same or more money as a freelancer than they did at their traditional job. These were individuals that leveraged the skills they had in order to create their own income and freedom. Freelancing is also great for the American economy. This freelancing workforce has added over $715 billion to the American economy. Freelancing has become an integral part of our economy and can shape the way we view work life balance – finding meaningful work that utilizes the skills we have while helping other and generating income to support ourselves.

"The price of anything is the amount of life you exchange for it." ~Henry David Thoreau

In her book *The MBA Bubble*, Mariana Zenetti stated:

If you want to be wealthy, at some moment of your life, you will have to create a source of income other than your salary. This is an evident and crushing reality: If you sell your time to others, you will quickly reach a limit in your capacity to generate income.

I think this is a reality that many American workers are facing, and it is why many are generating income through freelancing and other side hustles.

Remember the old saying "time is money"? This saying is just as wrong as telling people to "get good grades, go to college and get a good (traditional) job." Time is much more valuable than money, it's our most precious commodity because our lives depend on it. Money can come and go, but time is forever fleeting. How many years are we willing to exchange for a certain job? Is the price of a college degree worth the "life" we've exchanged for it? In any case, whether you have a degree or not, whether you have a white collar or blue-collar career, you can begin generating wealth (by freelancing or starting a business) and trading money for time (by investing). Freelancing could be considered a mild form of entrepreneurship. Starting a business would be diving into the waters of entrepreneurship, while freelancing gets your feet wet.

The Great Recession caused a dramatic shift in the American workforce. The shift seems to be towards income generating opportunities that may not require post-secondary education. According to a 2014 report from the U.S. Census Bureau, college enrollment declined for two straight years from 2012-2013. I'm not sure if this is a clear sign that the Education Bubble will soon burst, but I do think it shows young people's disenfranchisement with a system that has overpromised and under delivered.

Traditional jobs and the college degree aren't the safest bets. It's time for us to start doing the risky things, like pursuing our passion. Starting a business or freelancing is the result of passions being pursued. Our economy would be stronger if we had a nation of individuals who strived to do what they are most passionate about and skilled to perform. It's far better than having employees who are working jobs they don't care for. At the very least, people would be happy and enjoy what their doing.

Passion drives us, but we must consider the road ahead. If our chief aim is money, we aren't going to get farther than our bank accounts. If our chief aim is fame, we'll be crushed when we aren't fawned over. We need to ask ourselves why our existence matters to others, and how we can use our talents to help those around us.

As human beings, we are extremely relational; we're meant to live life in community. When we think of the most successful businesses, we find that they are the ones that help us connect with one another. Freelancing is primarily service-oriented. If you do decide to start a business/freelance, please consider your fundamental motivation. The next chapters are geared toward those who want to take the plunge into entrepreneurship. The good thing is you don't need business experience or a degree to pursue your passion. You just need to start.

7
ACTION!

The Great Divide

"In life and business, there are two cardinal sins: The first is to act without thought, and the second is to not act at all." - Carl Icahn, founder of Icahn Enterprises

As humans, we like to complicate things. Some of the most complex questions are solved by the simplest solutions. There's a big difference between successful entrepreneurs and everyone else. How did that happen? Some think its luck, a good idea, a "big break", that they were smarter, better, or richer than the Average Joe. As an entrepreneur, you should avoid thinking in terms of luck.

Luck is defined as a force that brings either good or bad fortune. Fortune is described as a personified power that unpredictably determines favorable or unfavorable events. If you can honestly look yourself in the mirror and say that you are in a situation because of an unpredictable outside force that is responsible for your life, then I would argue that you're fearful of responsibility. The only one who is responsible for where you are in life, where you will be, and what you will become is YOU. As an entrepreneur, luck should be annihilated from your vocabulary. You are accountable for every action you take. You can't play the blame game when things don't go your way. Now, I do believe God is the one who determines all things. He gives us passions and desires to pursue; fulfilling the purpose He has created us for. However, that doesn't absolve us from taking responsibility for our actions.

That was a tough lesson for me to learn. It's easy to blame others for your demise. No one wants to take responsibility for his or her actions, and I was no different. It's easy to blame colleges for charging high tuition, or jobs not being available because of corporate greed, or that "life isn't fair." I had to learn the hard way that the only person I could blame was me.

Being a college dropout, or working at a deadbeat job, was not going to stop me from making Don't Feed The Animals a success. I had to make decisions that would require sacrificing certain "luxuries", so that later on in life I wouldn't have to worry about not being able to afford the things I truly wanted. It was through accountability and responsibility that I made the sacrifices necessary to progress.

"Opportunity is missed by most because it is dressed in overalls and looks like work." - Thomas Alva Edison

"Big breaks" don't just happen, and opportunities are not just going to fall into your lap because you waited patiently for them. The good thing about opportunities is that they are endless. You just have to be willing to find them. Opportunities can also be created, so even if you've looked under every rock and turned every stone and couldn't find an opportunity, you can still create one. Opportunities are the foundation for success. Another crucial part of the foundation for success is an idea. An idea, combined with an opportunity to take that idea and make a profitable business, requires action. Without action, opportunities will pass you by as if you were a snail on the freeway. "Big breaks" do not occur by sitting and wishing for them to happen. When the opportunities to advance present themselves you must not only be prepared for them, you must also be willing and able to act on them. Otherwise, the opportunity is useless.

It's easy to expect things to simply happen in your favor, and have the world handed to you on a silver platter. It's a lot tougher to put in the work to achieve your goals and dreams. I can't say I never expected a "big break", or that I was never jealous of other people's success, or blamed their success on a stroke of luck. I finally realized that in order for me to improve the circumstances I was living in I needed to change my perception of the world. I had to accept responsibility for my actions, change my bad habits, and act on my good habits. I also had to accept that if I couldn't find an opportunity to use, I had to be very creative and think of ways to produce them.

Everyone who is capable of forming an idea is also capable of creating a good idea. Ideas, just like opportunities, are endless. Every idea won't be an epiphany moment, but the fact is that we think of hundreds of ideas, possibilities and scenarios each and every day. If you have come up with a good idea, you also have the potential to turn that idea into a profitable one. As an entrepreneur, you should not be afraid to take your idea and try to make a profit. You should have at least one good idea or think of a new idea each day. There is no excuse. Whether you're a CEO, high school student, cab driver, cashier, whatever, you have an idea that can generate income. So why isn't everyone sipping martinis in their private jets on their way to a party on a yacht near a private island? Action, or rather, inaction.

This is why this book isn't for everyone. The foundation to becoming an entrepreneur is action. This is what separates entrepreneurs from everyone else. They act on their ideas, while everyone else is hoping and waiting to get lucky. Everyone else is waiting for his or her "big break." Everyone else is too afraid to try. How many times have you heard people say, "that's so simple, I could of done that" when they refer to a new business, product or service? They deserve the response "so then why didn't you?" Of course you can add any type of degrading term at the end of that question, but let's take the high road. You may have heard people say "I had that same idea (insert however many minutes, days, months, years) ago" It's not enough to say you could've, should've or would've come up with a multi-billion dollar company.

One of the most important factors for starting a business is being a pioneer, one of the first to provide a certain service or product. Of course there are many other factors that we'll break down later, but being first, or one of the first, is vitally important for innovation. Now being first has its disadvantages. Your competition can exploit your weaknesses and try to create a rival product, and people are always reluctant to change, which could damage your start-up if your product is revolutionary. If you're a really good entrepreneur, you'll be able to adapt to the changes within your market so you can better serve your target audience. This is not your high school prom. It's not cool to show up late to the Profit Party because you thought people weren't ready, or you were scared because no one has done what you plan to do. The point is to start, make mistakes, and improve each step of the way. Act and you become a driving force, industry leader, revolutionary, and innovator. If you wait, you might as well write rough drafts of the fairy tales you'll tell your grandkids of how you almost created the next billion-dollar industry. You might want to add an apology note in there as well.

Now, the idea of a clothing brand is not revolutionary in any way shape or form. People have been wearing and selling clothes since the dawn of time. Hundreds of independent clothing brands are created each and every day. So how do you create a revolutionary product in a flooded market? One way is through branding. By shipping tees in custom packages, using unique business card ideas, and using designs that project our brand message, Don't Feed The Animals has positioned itself to stand out. Creating a brand with a cohesive message that resonates with people takes a lot of work. Each and every day you and I are flooded with ads and marketing strategies. At Don't Feed The Animals, we strive to create new ways to reach our target audience in the most effective and efficient way. Then our target audience becomes fans, loyal customers and followers of our ever-growing brand. Branding is a commitment. A commitment to excellence we've made at DFTA.

Blogging is another business you can start today, with no money down or risk of losing your investment. All you need is a computer and a passion. If you do decide to start writing, make sure your writing about something you're not only passionate about, but also would love to research and learn more about. You'd want to avoid writer's block as much as possible. Also, write about something you feel that would benefit others, a solution to a problem you feel that others need to hear. On my blog, thelionsshares.com, I write about budgeting, investing and wealth creation from the point of view of a Christian millennial in NYC. I believe this helps other millennials who are trying to find their purpose in the world build their financial future, as well as keep my wife and me accountable to our budget and financial planning. Whatever it is that you are most passionate about, you can start writing about it today. You have a unique point of view that others would be willing to hear.

8
ACT LIKE AN ENTREPRENEUR

The English word "entrepreneur" stems from the French word "entreprendre" which can be translated to mean 'to do something' or 'to undertake.' Many think entrepreneurs are a hybrid human species of risk takers/thrill junkies who are profit hungry and selfish. Some may think that they are rebellious and lazy because they don't want to conform to the ways of this wonderful society. Some even think it's impossible to become an entrepreneur and achieve great success. They aren't far off.

To become an entrepreneur, you need three things: an idea, an opportunity, and the courage to act on both. As I stated earlier, everyone has an idea, and opportunities are everywhere. You just have to find and create them, instead of waiting around for one to fall into your lap. If you have the courage to act on your idea, and create opportunities to grow and profit, then you will be well on your way into the successful entrepreneur hall of fame. It's not going to be easy, but it's also not impossible. Let's not overlook the fact that entrepreneurs are just human, not hybrid, super, or more capable than anyone else. They eat, breathe, and even bleed. I have the paper cuts to prove it. Many believe the life of an entrepreneur is filled with risks.

Entrepreneurs do take risks – everyone does, walking outside of your house is risky. Who knows if you'll get hit by a car or struck by lightning? You never know what can happen; risk is doing something without knowing or having a guaranteed outcome. Inaction is also a risk. You risk the chance of gaining something by being idle. You risk the opportunity to change your life. The goal is to take calculated risks. We'll get to risks later; just know that they are extremely important as far as entrepreneurship is concerned.

Starting a business from scratch is a major risk, especially if you have very little experience running a business. It's an uphill battle to say the least. You're taking a giant leap, stepping out of your comfort zone, and doing something that most people around you have never done.

When I first started DFTA clothing I had no prior business experience, but I was determined to learn as much as possible. Banks don't lend to teenagers without prior business experience, especially in a recession. I had to work jobs I had no interest in just to fund my business. I had to buy books on marketing, sales, leadership, economics, finance and branding so I could learn the skills to run my business. It was a major risk because I didn't know anyone who had started his or her own business and I was on my own. My first attempt at starting a clothing line failed. I learned a lot of "do's and don'ts" from that failure – such as the importance of a logo and that sales fuel a business – which helped me launch a better company the second time around. Even after the second launch, there were a series of opening and closing the business to improve DFTA.

I never gave up and continued to work on the many weaknesses my business had while improving my strengths. I was working a full time job, and then went home to work on my business until I fell asleep; I worked close to 100-hr weeks including weekends. Many friends and relatives didn't understand why I would take this kind of risk and I was even criticized at times for starting my own business. Everybody had an opinion, but I knew if I wanted to be successful, I had to listen to my gut and do everything I needed to create a successful and profitable business. Ultimately, the goal is to strive for excellence.

The word profit can trigger different emotions, depending on your point of view or your experience with how "profit" has been used to describe businesses. Some view it as a term for greed; others may see it as excess. For an entrepreneur, it should be viewed as essential. Without it, your business will fail. Trust me. If your business does not make money, (I don't care how many ways you try to spin it or present the numbers) you don't have a business. Businesses are designed to make money. Whatever you want to call your endeavor into entrepreneurship will fail. You must make whatever changes necessary to produce the maximum profit. It's your obligation as an entrepreneur to do so. Act and make profits, or stand there and watch your hopes and dreams crumble. I've seen the effects of action as well as inaction. There were plenty of times when I had to question whether or not I had a business.

Now I'm quite sure my accountant would not be happy with my general use of the word profit, because profit in accounting is the net gain, kept from revenue after all expenses have been paid. There are many successful businesses that have a "paper loss" (for accounting and tax purposes) yet they are generating cash. It is far beyond the scope of this book to debate different tax strategies or how this is possible, so talk to your accountant about those terms. You can also visit investopedia.com and other financial websites for different financial terms. For now, know that you want your business to generate cash and don't be afraid of profit. The point is you should make every effort to pursue excellence and create income. Don't let other people's perception of business, capitalism, or profit stop you from doing so.

Selfish people are not successful. Period. Life is a team sport. One person can't know everything; you can only go so far doing everything completely on your own. Eventually you're going to need to get by with a little help from your friends to succeed. Selfish people don't go anywhere in life. They may be able to take advantage of a couple of people for a short while, but no one likes a selfish person.

Some of the most successful entrepreneurs have created systems that help others. Systems that have revolutionized how we think, interact with each other, and survive. Many are also philanthropist and give to charities that do the same. As an entrepreneur, you must understand that some of the most successful companies are those that are socially conscious.

When we make a purchase, we want to know that our money goes beyond the pockets of the shareholders. We should strive to not only generate as much income as we can to feed our families – we should also use our income to benefit others. Profit for profit's sake is an unfulfilling goal.

I used to think I could do everything on my own, and if I didn't already know how to do it, I would learn. The problem is that time is just as valuable as money and I couldn't spend time learning things that I didn't necessarily need to know to run my business. Then I learned of a wonderful thing called outsourcing.

Outsourcing is when a company performs certain services for a business, at costs usually less than hiring someone internally to perform those services. I could pay other people to do tasks I wasn't able to do or that I wanted to avoid doing, such as taxes. I could focus my time on more important things such as improving my business system, marketing, and writing this book.

I'm also using other people's expertise and resources to improve my business. If I didn't have the money to outsource, I learned whatever skills I could so that my business continued to operate, saving money for future professional services.

Being a perfectionist is a detrimental trait for an entrepreneur to possess. Perfectionists don't allow anyone to do anything for them because they believe "if you want something done right, you need to do it yourself." Don't make this mistake. You will eventually need help to get your business off the ground. It was hard for me to trust others at first; I wanted to do everything on my own, and I saw no results. It wasn't until I stated delegating and outsourcing certain tasks that things really started to take off.

An entrepreneur is a person of action. How can a person be a lazy entrepreneur? It is not easy to be an entrepreneur. I'll repeat that. **It is not easy to be an entrepreneur.** I'll admit, there have been plenty of times that I've been unproductive. These times have been characterized by bouts of laziness, anxiety and unchecked frustration. Some people are afraid to take the plunge into entrepreneurship, and that's ok. Everyone isn't called to be an entrepreneur. There are vast differences between the responsibilities of an employee and those of an entrepreneur. One of the differences between an employee and an entrepreneur is that an employee has a set schedule; after they punch out they are no longer obligated to do the tasks that were required when they punched in. They can choose to work longer on a project, but it's not an obligation unless they accept certain responsibilities and take on more tasks. But it is still their choice. Entrepreneurship is a way of life. Even though you may not have a set schedule, you receive only what you put in. If you put in the work, you'll see results. They most likely will not be immediate, and the results may not be what you hoped for, but you *will* get results.

All the good and bad results that have come out of DFTA have been the product of what I put into my brand. Without sacrifice, there is no reward. It's your life. If you want to work to see results, then work and do whatever it takes to succeed. If you don't want to do the work, don't expect any handouts.

In order to become a successful entrepreneur, you must take every necessary step to achieve that goal and not expect the checks to start pouring in because you've simply thought of an amazing idea. That was something I learned: success is not automatic, it comes through hard work. Minimal effort will always yield lackluster results.

It takes time and sacrifice to see the benefits of your labor. People who aren't willing to work hard and sacrifice expect things to be handed to them. They expect things to happen; they think someone else will take care of them. Laziness is a trait that repels success. Lazy people expect things. Entrepreneurs do things.

Entrepreneurs are not "rebels without a cause." The cause is simple: The Mantra doesn't always work, so they take life into their own hands. There's more than one way around the track called success. The advice to pursue a degree is equivalent to taking a horse as your primary source of transportation. Many people still find success this way. It's worked even more successfully in the past, however things are different now. We don't need a faster horse. I'd much rather drive the car of entrepreneurship. We're in a time period that could be described as the "Golden Age of Entrepreneurial Endeavors." It's not only much easier to start a business (thanks to the internet) but the stigma surrounding business and entrepreneurship seems to be fading away.

If something is broke, I'm going to go out on a limb and suggest it should be fixed. If the system won't change, then you have to change. Change the way you think, live and learn. That takes action. Another difference between employees and entrepreneurs is their mindset. You must actively seek out new ways to learn. Here's a little known secret: college is not the only system or path for education. It also doesn't guarantee that you will learn a single thing.

I can't understand how a degree represents years of learning or that knowledge is retained through all those lovely extracurricular activities. Even without extracurricular activities, it's very difficult to retain information unless you are exposed to it frequently. I'm sure we're constantly exposing ourselves to the joys of radical mathematical expressions and important dates of the Revolutionary War. Seek out, ask questions, do something different.

Learning is active. I say that because once people are finished with formal schooling the drive to learn can slow down to a standstill. We should never feel as if we've finished learning. Learning is a lifelong process. As an entrepreneur, you should be actively learning all that you can about your customers, marketing, leadership, or any other subject that will help develop you or your business. You should actually learn something new every day rather than repeat a cliché phrase. Uneducated people are not successful and absolutely no one becomes successful by sitting on their hands. If you are not continuously applying yourself to the development of your mind, and acting on the things you learn, then throw all of your hopes and dreams of becoming wealthy and financially independent in the incinerator.

Action is what turns dreams into realities. It separates the wishers from the doers. It turns ideas into businesses. You can't be an entrepreneur without taking action. Simple as that. Take your idea, learn about your market, target audience, demographic and create a business to bring your idea to them. Getting started is the hardest and most important step for anything. There is a quote that goes, "I hear and I forget. I see and I remember. I do and I understand." Action brings understanding. By acting, concepts become clearer and tangible. Concepts are no longer theories; they become habits, and reference points for future decisions. Entrepreneurs understand that the best course of action is, well, acting. Even if a mistake is made, guess what, it's not the end of the world. Learning from mistakes is probably one of the best ways to learn. That's the only way I seem to learn. Strive to improve every day. Act on your idea. Don't wait, just do it.

Ask yourself these questions:

1. What am I most passionate about? Am I skilled at doing/creating something that revolves around my passion?

2. Would I enjoy doing/creating something around my strengths, even when times get difficult?

3. Would people find value in the things I do/create? Would they pay for it?

After you've answered these questions you'll have the framework for a business that is centered around your purpose. Start living out that purpose today!

9
THE ALTERNATIVE

No Means No

No one likes to be told what to do. I've even been characterized as stubborn because of this simple fact. A baby's first word is "no"; many teens go through a "rebellious phase." There is a constant struggle between those in positions of authority and those who aren't. No one can be *forced* to do anything. Period. Even if an action has a beneficial outcome, you can lead a horse to water, but it is ultimately the horse's decision to drink. Commands put us on the defense; they attack our pride. You can't shove your point down a person's throat; you must let them come to their own conclusions, or they will react negatively. We're defiant because we want to be our own leader. As humans, we take pride in our "free will." People want to feel as if they are in control, and by dictating what a person should or shouldn't do, or by insisting on a way of thinking of how society is "supposed" to work, will only make that person cling to their initial beliefs.

However, if you present your idea, request, or suggestion as an option instead of a demand, your chances of getting the message through to your audience will dramatically improve. Getting people to comply with what we would like them to do is about allowing the other person to feel as if they are coming to their own conclusions and making the decision. We relish the opportunity to explore different options, see multiple possibilities, and ultimately make our own decisions. As humans, we want to feel as if we are in control of our destiny, and we don't want our free will to be put on the back burner. Yet, there is one emotion that can crush the spirit of free will: fear.

Fear invokes an inexplicable terror that can prevent your brain from thinking rationally. The fear of spiders can make grown men squeal. The fear of the dark can paralyze you. The fear of public speaking is almost as frightening as the fear of death. These are examples of internal fears, and there are many external factors that can cause fear. Fear is used as a deterrent.

Certain fears are debilitating and it's important to take an inventory of what we're most afraid of. These fears can include being afraid of failure or of making a mistake. A fear of rejection is common among high school seniors hoping that they will be accepted into the college of their dreams. You may have a fear of your financial future if you don't have a "safe and secure" job that gives you a paycheck every other week. I can't say it's foolish to have these fears or any fears at all. Everyone has a fear, that's what makes us human.

Nevertheless, it would be extremely foolish to let fear inform the way you live. My fear of heights does not keep me from riding roller coasters. Fear does not have to control you, and you have to train yourself to think realistically instead of with fear. If you're not afraid to take a risk, here's a learning option you can pursue at any time, even during college.

Self-Education

Self-education may be one of the most underrated and overlooked learning options. If you put in the right amount of effort, it can be the most rewarding. I can't give you a list of things you must do, but I can suggest some things that can keep you on the right track for successful self-education. One thing is certain: you must be willing to read and work hard to apply what you've learned. Everything I've learned about business, I've read it either in a book or on the Internet, from trusted sources of course. I haven't put every single bit of useful information into practice, but I've given a solid effort to put as much of what I've learned to good use. Guess what? Everything you will ever need to know is probably in a book anyway. Last time I checked, professors teach out of textbooks, so why not skip the middlemen and teach yourself?

One of the hardest and most important qualities that are

essential to everything in life is focus. I'm sure you have a vision of where you want to be. Keep that vision clear in your mind and focus on that goal. For many, financial freedom is one of the main goals they set for themselves. A lack of focus can derail you from the financial freedom express. The good thing is that focus can be created and built upon.

All you need to do is devote consistent time to learning skills that will benefit you in the long run. It doesn't necessarily have to be a daily routine, just as long as you are actively taking charge of your education. It would be futile to set a strict daily course study for yourself if two weeks later you lose the focus on your education. You have to be willing to change your way of thinking, and taking on an attitude that will create the determination to achieve your goals. A lack of focus will utterly destroy your dreams and goals. It's the same concept of a dieter who wants to lose weight. Unless they change their method of thinking their efforts will be futile, and in a week they will be back to their old habits. The change has to be internal for it to take full effect. You'll need discipline to train yourself to stay focused. Easier said than done, I know, but it is crucial to your success. Focus turns dreams into realities. Start focusing on certain tasks for a set amount of time. Once you feel comfortable with this, increase the amount of time. You'll be amazed at how productive you will become. This method has helped me focus and finish projects, which is something I still struggle with.

The desire to learn is the foundation for self-education. Humans have an innate desire to learn. We are fascinated by the world around us and want to learn how everything works and is governed. There is a passion and thirst for knowledge that is within all of us. But after years of being ordered how and what to learn, the desire can fade. Those who graduate college can lose that desire once they get their degree. I'm not saying this is always the case, but it's easy to stop striving forward if we believe we have "arrived." Our accomplishments can cause us to stop creating new goals to reach. Some may feel that they have reached the apex of learning in their field of study and no longer need to learn because their "advanced degree" is an indicator of all their knowledge. A college degree isn't a barometer of a person's intelligence. If you are not continuously learning, what you've learned is irrelevant.

"In times of change, learners inherit the earth, while the learned find themselves beautifully equipped to deal with a world that no longer exists." - Erik Hoffer.

You must be eager to adapt and desire to learn in this ever-changing world. You alone are responsible for your life. You are the only person that decides whether or not you learn and grow. Passion should drive you to learn. Focus should direct what and how you learn. Clarity of purpose will help remind you of why you've pursued self-education.

Once you have the desire to learn and focus on what you want to learn, the next step is to start. The hardest thing to do is to start. Many people get overwhelmed and fail to even start a project. It's hard because you may not even know where to start. So here are four resources that can help you get started on your plunge into entrepreneurship: book stores, Google, Amazon, and the library. I've used all of these resources and I wouldn't recommend them if they didn't work for me. It's not a groundbreaking concept.

This is the Information Age. Information is everywhere. No matter what you plan on studying, there are countless authors who have written about it. The information you need isn't hiding under a rock; a quick trip to the library, or local bookstore will prove how available and accessible information is. There is also this wonderful thing called the Internet; consider it your genie in a bottle. Of course you can't believe every single thing you read on the Internet, but I'm sure with the right amount of effort to search for the answers, a little discretion, and with some deductive reasoning you'll be able to discover valuable information.

iTunes U is an incredible resource for those who want information taught at the college level, without paying college prices to have it. In fact the content on iTunes U is FREE. The information you want on almost any subject is right at your fingertips. Information is almost as valuable as money.

These classes aren't accredited, but if you're receiving the same information taught in classes most people would dream of attending, at no cost, does paying for the information make sense? Should the piece of paper a college degree is printed on be more valuable than the time and money spent on the **same information**?

Another invaluable resource you can use is Google Scholar; it is the best way to read peer reviewed articles from some of the brightest minds on the planet. These aren't sketchy Internet sites. There is access to information on any subject you're looking for (some articles need to be purchased for a small fee). The same academic journals you would have to cite and reference in research papers are a Google search away.

It's just a matter of how badly you want to pursue your own education. There are few things that can stop a locomotive in motion. However, that same train will not move if you place small rocks in front of the wheels while it is at a standstill. One of these rocks that stop many people is fear. But you already know this; so then what are you waiting for?

Same Difference

Education is the key to your success. Contrary to popular belief, formal schooling is not the only path to being educated. I hope you have looked over the lists of the entrepreneurs without a college degree. Some achieved certain levels of success without a high school diploma. Some may say that "they got lucky" or those were very unique individuals and very few people can accomplish what they've achieved. Others foolishly say it can't be done. Well, it can obviously be done. What made those entrepreneurs unique is that they actually put their mind to achieving something and sought the ways to achieve it. You should ask, "What did they do to achieve this success?"

I'll tell you what they didn't do: they didn't sulk or let

circumstances dictate how their life will be lived. Instead they sought the resources they need to start their businesses, and then actually started their business. They didn't complain about how unfair life is since they didn't have the education provided by formal schooling, but instead they taught themselves. So why did they forgo the "opportunity" of pursuing a college education? Let's speculate.

"If you don't design your own life plan, chances are you'll fall into someone else's plan. And guess what they have planned for you? Not much." -Jim Rohn

There are many differences in the thinking processes of the owner of a company and the employee of that same company. One sought to create a company, be more responsible and is solely accountable for their success. The other believed that it is safer to live depending on a paycheck, and that their employer will take care of them. Formal schooling teaches you to become an employee, to follow a path mapped out for you. Successful entrepreneurs create their own path. Entrepreneurs start businesses, while everyone else works for them. There is no college course that teaches you how to start a business, how to be an entrepreneur, or how to create a system for your business. In recent years colleges have offered courses in entrepreneurship, but I don't think business acumen is acquired in a classroom.

Entrepreneurship is born through an inner desire to create, and the action to act on that desire. A college course can't teach you any specifics about YOUR business. This is because every business is different – from its legal structure to its product or service. Business Management only teaches you how to become a manager of a system made by someone else, and that someone else is an entrepreneur. A degree in business management is almost useless in starting your own business. I say almost because you can at least gain *some* insight into how a business should work. The degree won't tell you what products/services consumers demand, or how difficult the road will be.

Anything worth pursuing will have its difficulties. Anything worth having will require sacrifice. If it were easy to create a successful business then every person on the planet would have at least one. Starting a business gives you the opportunity to blaze your own trail. Of course there is a huge risk involved, and you may even fail, but you can't give up if this is an option you really want to pursue. Creating a successful business will be very rewarding, but it's not a get rich quick scheme – it takes time and dedication. Successful entrepreneurs see an opportunity, formulate an idea, analyze the risk involved, and then act. They want to be free from a boss hovering over them. They do not want to be complacent and do what everyone else does. They choose not to follow The Mantra and create their own path. There is a deep desire in entrepreneurs to follow their passion and do what they want to do.

Trust me when I tell you that entrepreneurship is not a get rich quick scheme. I poured thousands of dollars into Don't Feed The Animals before I made my first sale! DFTA at one point was nothing more than a screen printer in my room, a laptop, and a kitchen table to sew and print my t-shirts. I joked that my shirts were literally made in the kitchen, and when I cooked up a new idea I was probably washing dishes too. It took a lot of hard work to get my business to where it is now and I understand it will take even more work to continue to progress. Entrepreneurship is a marathon, not a 40-yard dash.

I never liked school, except maybe kindergarten. One of the functions of formal schooling is to train you to become a good employee and thus a functioning member of society. The system is designed to punish mistakes. You must follow everything the teacher dictates without question. If you don't perform well on tests, don't finish assignments, or do exactly what the teacher says, then you fail. Of course you need to be respectful of your teachers (I'm not declaring anarchy) but the way in which mistakes are dealt with is completely detrimental to the way we learn. Students are made to feel ashamed when they make a mistake, as if everything they do must be perfect. When you graduate and enter the workforce, mistakes are avoided like a plague. Whatever guidelines your company gives you must be followed, or you are threatened with unemployment. There is no room for creativity, and you are at the mercy of your boss.

However, mistakes are essential. No one learned how to walk, eat, or perform basic functions without making a mistake. We actually learn more by making mistakes than by getting everything right. Getting something right is obviously important and even if you make a mistake, the end result should be solving a problem. But by being wrong, we learn what doesn't work and that leads us to find out what does work.

Not learning from mistakes is extremely dangerous. Mistakes help us change and adapt our way of thinking, which ultimately leads to growth. If you keep doing the same thing with no change in results, then you are the engaging in definition of insanity. It is insane to think that The Mantra still works.

The National Association of Colleges and Employers stated that only 24.4 percent of 2010 graduates who applied for a job were employed immediately after graduation. This was actually an improvement from 19.7 percent in 2009. There's been a shift in how success will be obtained. In 2014, underemployment is the new norm for college graduates. According to a study conducted by the Federal Reserve Bank of New York, 33% of college graduates are underemployed – **working jobs that do not require a college degree**. You must adapt. Either waste 2-4 years of your life hoping for a job that will most likely not exist, or actively work on educating yourself so you can survive in this ever-changing world.

Extinct

By now I hope you've come to the realization that the old way of thinking is dead, and by following The Mantra you may suffer the same fate. But there is another dying breed I briefly mentioned earlier: creativity. Formal schooling kills creativity. It traps you into thinking a certain way and to follow a predesigned trail. If you give a child an assignment to write a one-page paper on a topic, the child will resist. Tell the same child to write about any topic they choose and I'm sure the child will produce more than one page of work.

Yes, there is a curriculum that has to be followed but we are innately eager to express ourselves. Give a child a creative outlet instead of constantly giving them mandatory assignments. Mandatory and mundane tasks cause children to misbehave when they are not given opportunities to express themselves. No one thoroughly enjoys being told what to do. Creativity allows us to exercise our brain and do something we want to do. It fuels us to be different, setting ourselves apart from everyone else.

For thousands of years people didn't go to college. Until 500 years ago people simply pursued their passions; they created businesses or worked in industries where their skills and passions aligned. Our current education system fails creative thinkers. We steer children away from creative outlets into highly esteemed subjects, particularly math and science. I'm not saying math and science are bad; they just aren't the culmination of human intelligence. Our society is more afraid of these children growing up and not having a job, rather than being terrified of destroying their creativity. We're keeping them from pursuing their passion and purpose. Quite frankly, we've disregarded them as individuals.

Sir Ken Robinson says, "We are educated out of creativity." Although intelligence is multifaceted, we've placed a hierarchy on each facet. Math and science are at the height, followed by languages, history and the other humanities; art is last on our intelligence value system. Creativity, therefore, is also undervalued in our educational system. I don't intend to bash other subjects and say they are uncreative. As a person who is fascinated by numbers, I'm fully aware that there have been many creative thinkers in math, science, and language disciplines; we've all heard of Albert Einstein and William Shakespeare. However, art seems to be engulfed in creative expression. Unfortunately, our education system isn't interested in fostering creative expression in any field. Mistakes aren't tolerated, and perfection is the only option. Conformity to the "norm" is the only goal. Individuality isn't celebrated unless its been sanitized to certain parameters. Our society can't tolerate creativity because it's too radical. But, this wasn't always the case.

The reason why we direct children to college and to certain majors (with certain careers in mind) is because we have been educated out of creativity. There is only one clear path to success in America. That's to go to school, get good grades, go to college and find a job. We completely disregard the fact that higher education is a relatively new phenomenon that started with a drastically different purpose than what we experience today. However, business has, and will continue to be, the driving force for success in our economy as a whole and for individuals. Each and every type of field (including the arts) involves business. Business is connected to everything we do.

Artists don't have to starve: they can sell their art! They can become art curators, or producers of music, or dancers, actors, writers, etc. We've stopped being creative about the way we can express ourselves, so we've also stopped being creative about how we could support ourselves financially. Working for someone else isn't the only way to support yourself. How do you think your boss (if he's the business owner) supports himself? We've stopped thinking through the ways we can use business in every field because we've been taught to focus on being an employee rather than a business owner.

"A business has to be involving, it has to be fun, and it has to exercise your creative instincts." -Richard Branson

Entrepreneurs are creative. They find ways to differentiate their products in flooded markets, find innovative ways of doing things or create a new product/service. They adapt to the problems and changes of the world and are able to benefit because of their open-minded thinking and creativeness. While many see what can't be done or that something is impossible, entrepreneurs create a way to make it possible. Boring just simply doesn't sell. Entrepreneurs solve problems.

Those who are bold enough to be creative, to challenge the world around them, and to change themselves will prosper. I mentioned earlier that a clothing brand is not a new idea. Retail clothing has to be one of the most flooded markets – everyone has a clothing brand now. For DFTA to survive, I had to think of creative ways to differentiate my product from the masses.

I did this through custom labels, packaging, and unique designs. I also had think of creative ways to market and distribute my products so that people can learn about Don't Feed The Animals and place orders. I can't tell you my marketing methods, otherwise I'd lose business, but I had to continuously change my marketing so I could continue to create customers.

Creative people bring a breath of fresh air in a world filled with the average. Why is it that people are in such awe of those who achieve incredible success in their respective fields? Is it because they are special? Not at all! Anyone can be creative; all it takes is a willingness to think. Unfortunately, as Henry Ford so perfectly stated: **"Thinking is the hardest work there is, which is probably the reason why so few engage in it."**

Napoleon Hill named his book THINK *and Grow Rich* for a reason. Freedom to pursue your passion is another species on the verge of extinction. When you enter college, you are forced to declare a major, and that decision will determine not only the courses you study, but also how the rest of your life will be lived. This can be one of the scariest decisions a person can make, knowing that this decision could ultimately determine who they will become.

Yes, you can change your major, but not after spending time studying for a different one. And time is more valuable than money. The decision also has to take into account the current job market, competition for jobs, and salary. Once you make this decision, you must study the required courses, including those you dislike or feel you may never need. Once you graduate, you have an obligation to yourself. That obligation is to find a job that is related to your major, otherwise the time you put into studying and getting good grades is completely worthless. We have to think very hard about why we are either going or sending people to college. If it's simply for education, we could definitely find more cost effective ways to educate ourselves. If it's simply to find a job, then we need to be sure that the degree is a necessary step toward that goal. If you can't find a job, or if you find a job that is unrelated to your degree, then the accomplishment of graduating from college is insignificant. That is the bottom line.

Your ROI, or return on investment, is zero, or rather negative because you've lost valuable time. Of course, you did earn a nice chunk of debt, but let's get back to choices. Let's say that you are one of the very fortunate college graduates that are able to find a job relevant to your major. Is it time to pop open the champagne? Not so fast; job security is a myth. So let's say the most horrible thing in the world happens: you lose your job. Now what do you do? Unless you have versatile skills that can be used in various fields, and the experience that demonstrates a mastery of those skills, then you will have a difficult time trying to gain employment. An accounting degree is worthless if the only jobs available are in the psychology field and vice versa. This is because you have to become a specialist in your field to earn a larger salary, and the more you hone your skills for a specific field, the less likely you will be able to prove that your skills are applicable to a different field. You are left with no options.

With self-education, you are the pilot. You determine what you want to study, how frequently you study, and when and where you want to study. You always have the choice to change what you want to do. If you are able to develop skills that can be demonstrated in front of a potential employer, then that is more valuable than a piece of paper. But this is also a double-edged sword. It is a lot more work and a lot tougher to train yourself, especially if you are used to being taught by someone else all your life. It's a much tougher, but potentially more rewarding road. If you are willing and able to educate yourself, and your desire to succeed and fear of the status quo are fueling you, success is not too far away. All it takes is persistence and a willingness to continue learning and improving.

The life of an entrepreneur isn't filled with rainbows, unicorns, and cotton candy. It is hard work, and some people may not want to put in the effort to achieve success. It's your choice, but how many people can say that they are completely responsible for their lives? That they determine how long they work a day? How successful they will be? That doesn't answer to a boss but instead call the shots?

10
ENTREPRENEUR 101

No book, college, or course can give you a step-by-step guide on how to become an entrepreneur. I'd be a fool to try. Being an entrepreneur is about creating your own path, making mistakes and learning from them.

So you'll determine what you will have to do to become a successful business owner. What I can do is present some of the attributes of an entrepreneur. I've pointed you in the direction you should take to start your self-education. There is a common theme that links many entrepreneurs, so we'll try to dissect what the foundation is to become one.

I Think, Therefore I Am

This is a no brainer. Entrepreneurs must be able to think on their feet; otherwise their business ventures will fail. There are two ways of thinking: rationally and emotionally. There are also two types of knowledge: codified knowledge and tacit knowledge. We'll start with the differences in thinking and then we'll review the knowledge that stems from each one.

How you think is everything. Many people cannot tell the difference between an emotional decision and a rational decision. People who are controlled by their emotions make decisions based on impulses rather than reviewing the options presented to them. They may take out a loan to buy a bigger house, a new car, take out an extra line of credit to go on a shopping spree, or may go to college because they "feel" it would lead to a "safe and secure" job. These people let the way they feel, or what others feel they should do dictate their decisions. They follow the crowd instead of doing their research and doing things differently. They then pass on emotional advice to their children and to others, thus creating a vicious cycle.

As an entrepreneur you should be aware of what is

influencing your decision making process: your brain or your heart. The heart is deceiving, and if you base your thinking on what may "seem like a good idea", then you're setting yourself up for disaster. An example of this is impulse spending. Impulse spending is based on emotions, and your emotions will bankrupt you. However, by using your brain and thinking before each decision, you will realize the consequences involved with emotional decision-making. Humans are very emotional, and it's difficult to make the right choices without becoming emotionally attached to a situation. I'm not a robot, and I wouldn't advise you to be one either, but it does take a little effort to settle your emotions, clear your mind, and make the appropriate decision. Rational thinking and thought patterns are crucial for an entrepreneur.

Successful entrepreneurs are in control of their emotions. Many people allow their emotions to control them. Entrepreneurs think positively, and don't let their fears control them. They look at a situation, see different outcomes and select the best solution. Many people think in terms of "can't." "I can't learn, can't succeed, can't do this, can't do that" when in reality they are simply afraid of uncertainty. By saying that they "can't" achieve or accomplish a task, they have defeated themselves. Entrepreneurs think, "How can I do this? What can be done?" They ask questions, which opens the mind to find a solution. Asking questions jumpstart the brain and promotes rational thinking. "Why?" is one of the most profound things a person can ask. It shows that a person is searching for purpose and is using logic to find it. Questions challenge us to find answers and seek knowledge.

Similarly, there are two types of knowledge: explicit knowledge and tacit knowledge.

Tacit knowledge is knowledge gained through experience and observation. Explicit knowledge is knowledge that can be quantified and articulated. For example, we can observe gravity when we see things continuously fall to the ground. We know that every time something falls it doesn't stay suspended in air, and this type of knowledge is called tacit knowledge. When Sir Isaac Newton continued to observe apples falling from trees and discovered the Universal Law of Gravitation (the force of gravity equals the mass of an object times the acceleration of the object), he used explicit knowledge to convey his findings.

Explicit knowledge can become tacit knowledge (and vice versa). We wouldn't say we perform everyday tasks such as brushing our teeth at a certain time as a quantifiable (explicit) knowledge; we may have learned at one time to brush our teeth but now we do it out of habit (tacit). We no longer contemplate the steps to brush our teeth; we simply know what to do. Knowledge learned explicitly is the foundation to the habits we form tacitly. For example, many people have little to no knowledge about certain concepts, such as finance, and therefore have not developed a stable financial foundation. This leads to bad habits and poor money management. Since they haven't learned the quantifiable rules about money, their experience with money will continue to be a poor one. Having financial literacy can mitigate this problem.

It is solely the responsibility of the person seeking knowledge to obtain the knowledge they need to succeed. The good news is that knowledge learned can be obtained in many ways. You can learn from your parents, from school, books, the Internet, a story, lectures, and the list goes on. There is unlimited *potential* to how much explicit knowledge an individual can gain. Explicit knowledge can be acquired, but it can also be lost and forgotten. Explicit knowledge is a straightforward concept. It is what we have been taught through others and the world around us.

But learning is only one aspect of knowledge. There is a big difference between "knowing" and "doing". You can know the concept of saving money, know the benefits of saving money, and understand that saving money is a great option when it comes to your long term goals of starting a business or retiring. Yet, until you actually start saving money and become a habitual saver, "knowing" is pointless. True understanding is achieved by action and creating habits. The way that explicit and tacit knowledge interacts is very important. What you learn today can lead to good or bad habits in the future; what you do with what you learn can decide how successful you become. You can learn all the terms, trading techniques, investment vehicles and everything else there is to know about the stock market, but if you haven't invested a single dollar into the market, what's the point of having all that knowledge? Knowledge alone won't make money, proper application of that knowledge will.

College graduates who are either unemployed, underemployed, or are working at a job unrelated to their major, are filled with important but worthless information. Having a degree in aviation is pointless if the only jobs available are in retail. Although many of these "highly educated" graduates have a degree to display in their parents living room, they lack the most important skill: experience. Experience can be gained by anyone. All you have to do is take the knowledge you've learned, act on it, create habits (preferably good habits), and voila! Instant experience. In business, experience beats a degree every time.

Actually, experience is more valuable than a degree in any circumstance. A degree demonstrates explicitly learned knowledge; experience incorporates both explicit and tacit knowledge. Last time I checked, there was no degree for experience, or a college that gives you the experience an employer is looking for. There are internships, but otherwise there is no other real experience in the field. I would rather see what a person has accomplished than hear a person eloquently ramble on about what they plan to do.

Show Me the Money

Entrepreneurs start businesses. Businesses are created to serve the entrepreneur. Businesses create money. That's the bottom line. If you're business doesn't make money, you will fail. Guaranteed. There is no grey area when it comes to a business' purpose in generating income. Nevertheless, there is no reason you have to be cutthroat. Many successful entrepreneurs achieved great wealth by being interested in others, being approachable and being people oriented. In fact, if you create a business from your passion, instead of simply for the money, your passion could keep you from giving up too soon. This is especially important in the beginning stages of your business, when your business is most likely not generating income. People will be more willing to give you their money if they trust you and can identify with you. People like people who are like them. I wouldn't want to spend my money on a product if the customer service is poor. I especially wouldn't give my money to someone who didn't like me. It is in your best interest to be interested in people because at the end of the day they are the ones who will decide whether or not they will buy your product or service.

Businesses are designed to make profits. As an entrepreneur, you have the obligation to create a business that will produce maximum profit. If you feel uneasy about the word "profit" then you had better get rid of that queasiness. Without it, your business has no chance to succeed. If you are afraid to profit because you think you will become a greedy goblin, consider this: what if your business manufactures lifeboats and preservers? Without profits, you can't produce efficiently; you won't be able to create a sufficient amount of boats made with quality materials, and your business will have a hard time paying workers who need to feed their families. And we haven't even talked about you and your need to keep your family financially afloat. Now, if you reflect on the consequences of not seeking profits, you may cost the lives of those on your boats, the lives of your workers, and the lives of the members in your family. Whether you would like to accept it or not, profits are necessary. Of course, businesses created for the **sole purpose** of generating a profit are unfruitful and unfulfilling. Profit shouldn't be avoided, but it also shouldn't be the only thing we strive for.

To stay in business, you must create cash flow. Cash flow is the difference between cash coming into the business and cash going out of the business. Cash flow is the lifeblood for any business. Without cash, a business can't sustain itself. If there's no cash, a business can't pay employees, it can't buy new products or continue their services, and ultimately it will not survive. Cash is King, and without it there is no kingdom, i.e. your business. Controlling the amount of cash coming into and out of your business is one of the main priorities of an entrepreneur. It's also important to take the same approach with your personal finances. You'll want more cash flowing into your business (and into your home) than out of your business. The more cash your business has, the more opportunities you'll have to grow your business.

How do you create cash flow? Find customers for your business. Customers are the heart of every single business. Without buyers, there's nothing to sell. How do you find customers? Marketing. Marketing is misunderstood. Many people assume that selling, advertising, and promoting are interchangeable terms that describe marketing. However, marketing is the process of creating and keeping customers. It should also be noted that the process never ends; selling, advertising and promoting are only cogs within the larger process of marketing. They are vital parts to marketing, but they are only parts.

Marketing is the vein that finds customers, thus creating cash flow. Successful entrepreneurs are expert marketers. They create a marketing system that finds customers, generates cash flow, and then continues to find customers. Without a solid marketing plan, a business will not create a large enough customer base to support it. The business must either continue to find new customers or create brand loyalty through repeat customers. Part of the cash flow from these customers must go back into your marketing budget. Marketing is the key to creating and maintaining a successful business. I had no idea what marketing was, but I knew that I had to learn about it in order to be successful. I've read books by expert marketers like Seth Godin, Dan S. Kennedy, and Donald Trump to learn and utilize the techniques they employ. I highly recommend that you do the same.

Study Money

Money is a concept. Money is an idea. There's more than one way to "make" money. All it takes is a little creativity. Creativity will lead to opportunities to really "make" money, instead of "earning" money. To develop this creativity and start searching for these opportunities, you'll need financial education. Financial education is necessary for everyone, and is sadly not taught in school. It can be learned but more importantly, you must continue to learn about it. The foundation for your financial education is the understanding of the difference between an asset and a liability.

The balance sheet for a business, as well as for your personal finances, will show your assets and liabilities. Assets generate income (whether it's recurring income or one time income when the asset is sold) while liabilities generate expenses. The goal is to increase your assets and decrease your liabilities. The difference between your assets and liabilities is your net worth (Assets - Liabilities = Net Worth). Assets generate wealth and allow you to obtain more assets, while liabilities take away your opportunities by taking your money. Since financial literacy isn't taught in schools, many people are incapable of managing their money. They buy liabilities and wonder why they aren't getting ahead in life. They increase their expenses and force themselves to live paycheck to paycheck, instead of buying income-generating assets.

On an income statement (both for business and personal finances), you'll find the difference between revenue and expenses. The difference between revenue and expenses is your profit or net income (revenue – expenses = net income). As a stated earlier, liabilities increase your expenses, which will decrease your profit, while assets generate income/revenue, which increases your profit (or net income). The cash flow statement is the same as I mentioned previously. It is the difference between the amount of cash going into your business (or personal accounts) and the amount that goes out (Cash In – Cash Out = Cash Flow). If there is more cash coming in, then cash flow is positive. If there is more coming out, then cash flow is negative. We intuitively know that cash flow should be positive, although our bank statements may paint a different picture. For personal finances, the income and cash flow statement will almost be identical. Below are sample balance sheets, income and cash flow statements for reference:

Example Company
Balance Sheet
December 31, 2014

ASSETS			LIABILITIES	
Current assets			Current liabilities	
Cash	$	2,100	Notes payable	$ 5,000
Petty cash		100	Accounts payable	35,900
Temporary investments		10,000	Wages payable	8,500
Accounts receivable - net		40,500	Interest payable	2,900
Inventory		31,000	Taxes payable	6,100
Supplies		3,800	Warranty liability	1,100
Prepaid insurance		1,500	Unearned revenues	1,500
Total current assets		89,000	Total current liabilities	61,000
Investments		36,000	Long-term liabilities	
			Notes payable	20,000
Property, plant & equipment			Bonds payable	400,000
Land		5,500	Total long-term liabilities	420,000
Land improvements		6,500		
Buildings		180,000		
Equipment		201,000	Total liabilities	481,000
Less: accum depreciation		(56,000)		
Prop, plant & equip - net		337,000		
Intangible assets			STOCKHOLDERS' EQUITY	
Goodwill		105,000	Common stock	110,000
Trade names		200,000	Retained earnings	229,000
Total intangible assets		305,000	Less: Treasury stock	(50,000)
			Total stockholders' equity	289,000
Other assets		3,000		
Total assets		$ 770,000	Total liabilities & stockholders' equity	$ 770,000

The notes to the sample balance sheet have been omitted.

Sample Products Co.
Income Statement
For the Five Months Ended May 31, 2014

Sales		$100,000
Cost of goods sold		75,000
Gross profit		25,000
Operating expenses		
Selling expenses		
Advertising expense	2,000	
Commissions expense	5,000	7,000
Administrative expenses		
Office supplies expense	3,500	
Office equipment expense	2,500	6,000
Total operating expenses		13,000
Operating income		12,000
Non-Operating or other		
Interest revenues		5,000
Gain on sale of investments		3,000
Interest expense		(500)
Loss from lawsuit		(1,500)
Total non-operating		6,000
Net Income		$ 18,000

Example Corporation
Statement of Cash Flows
For the Year Ended December 31, 2013

Cash Flow from Operating Activities

Net income	$23,000
Add: depreciation expense	4,000
Increase in accounts receivable	(6,000)
Decrease in inventory	9,000
Decrease in accounts payable	(5,000)
Cash provided (used) in operating activities	25,000

Cash Flow from Investing Activities

Capital expenditures	(28,000)
Proceeds from sale of property	7,000
Cash provided (used) by investing activities	(21,000)

Cash Flow from Financing Activities

Borrowings of long-term debt	10,000
Cash dividends	(5,000)
Purchase of treasury stock	(8,000)
Cash provided (used) by financing activities	(3,000)

Net increase in cash	1,000
Cash at the beginning of the year	1,200
Cash at the end of the year	$ 2,200

The balance sheet, income and cash flow statements are the

foundation to your financial success. It's alarming to think that in the last three paragraphs, you've been given more of a financial education than most high schools and colleges require. To be fair, there are personal finance courses you can take in college, but the fact that they aren't required classes (when you'll be dealing with financial matters for the rest of your life) is absurd. We need to start learning and teaching youth about the more important and practical aspects of life.

Money is about leverage. The more leverage you have, the more opportunities you may have. Also, depending on how you use leverage, you can multiply your money and create wealth with smaller amounts of money than you would think. Leverage is a concept that is slightly more advanced than the straightforward financial statements described above. Nevertheless, it's a topic that an aspiring entrepreneur should do further research on. Leverage is measured in debt and equity. Debt and equity determine ownership. Debt means that you owe others money, and don't have ownership of something. Equity on the other hand indicates that you have at least part ownership of something. For example, let's say you own your home, 20% of it is in the form of equity while 80% is in the form of debt. If you forget to pay off your debt, you'll understand who really owns you and your property.

Taxes are a form of debt. It's also a liability. I say this because you pay this expense to the government, and tax evasion is illegal. You are "indebted" to the government because they provide laws that govern and maintain society. Tax is a liability because it takes money out of your pocket before you even cash your check. If we look at this debt as a tool for determining ownership, the government owns you, or at least your money, from January to April (for those in tax brackets of 25% or more as of 2015). The amount of taxes you pay throughout a year is equivalent to working solely to pay taxes for these four months. The more earned income you make, the more taxes are taken out. So a higher income doesn't *necessarily* guarantee a better quality of life. This is partly due to taxes.

Being able to reduce your tax liabilities can greatly increase your chances of generating wealth that you can use to fund your business. Higher income is not the answer to your money problems.

In 2015, the IRS tax brackets for individual taxpaying employees were as follows:

If Taxable Income is between:	Tax Payable is:
$0 - $9,225	10% of taxable income
$9,226 - $37,450	$922.50 + 15% of the amount over $9,225
$37,451 - $90,750	$5,156.25 + 25% of the amount over $37,450
$90,751 - $189,300	$18,481.25 + 28% of the amount over $90,750
$189,301 - $411,500	$46,075.25 + 33% of the amount over $189,300
$411,501 - $413,200	$119,401.25 + 35% of the amount over $411,500
$413,201 +	$119,996.25 + 39.6% of the amount over $413,200

The Corporate Tax rates for taxable income were as follows:

$0 - $50,000	15% of taxable income
$50,000 - $75,000	$7,500 + 25% of the amount over $50,000
$75,000 - $100,000	$13,750 + 34% of the amount over $75,000
$100,000 - $335,000	$22,250 + 39% of the amount over $100,000
$335,000 - $10,000,000	$113,900 + 34% of the amount over $335,000
$10,000,000 - $15,000,000	$3,400,000 + 35% of the amount over $10,000,000
$15,000,000- $18,333,333	$5,150,000 +38% of the amount over $15,000,000
$18,333,333 +	35% of taxable income

In almost every tax bracket, businesses have more favorable

tax rates. The government essentially has a double tax on high-income earners who took out student loans (read chapter 3). Pursuing a higher income via a college degree will not only result in being placed in a higher tax bracket, but will most likely have you paying 4-6% interest payments on your student loans (which I believe is a double tax on our income). The federal government will always promote the college education system because it is it's most profitable enterprise. The government will continue to promote college education – and student loans to pay for it – as a means to a better quality of life. It then encourages individuals to pursue jobs with high wages in order to tax them at a higher rate.

To create wealth for yourself, the best option you have is to start a business. Businesses are taxed based on their taxable income, not by the revenue or cash flow they generate. Without going into too much detail, it is possible for a business to generate positive cash flow, while showing a taxable loss. If a business shows a taxable loss on their tax forms, they don't have to pay income tax since they didn't *technically* generate an income to tax. There are books that have been written about the difference between taxable income and cash flow for businesses, and how taxes can be avoided by owning a business with a particular formation (C-corp, S-corp, LLC, etc.), so I'm not going to get into all of the different nuances to tax laws here. The point is, that higher income as an individual isn't the solution to your problems. Being financially savvy, and owning a business, is the answer.

Higher income for individuals can also lead to higher spending habits. If a person makes a million dollars a year and spends a million dollars a year, they are in the same boat as the person who makes minimum wage and spends their whole paycheck each week. To create wealth, you don't need a higher income. There needs to be a shift in mentality. An entrepreneur cannot be consumer minded, where they spend all their money on things to satisfy wants or desires. They need to delay self-gratification and make sacrifices to cut their spending habits.

They should save money so that it could either be used for their business, or for investing in income-generating assets. Your mindset should shift from doing whatever it took to buy that item you "needed", to doing whatever it takes to be successful. All it takes is a little financial education to realize that by saving money, opportunities to make money suddenly become available. The opportunities are there; it's your responsibility to generate wealth.

I used to have the bad habit of collecting sneakers. When I began working at 16 the majority of my paycheck was spent on sneakers, or on outfits to match them. I must have spent thousands of dollars on things I don't even have anymore. It wasn't until I dropped out of college at 19 that I realized enough was enough. I didn't want to spend any more money on clothes and sneakers that kept me from being financially stable. I wanted to be the one selling the clothes to make money, so I started selling my unwanted sneakers and clothes on eBay. I finally woke up and realized that spending everything I had was going to get me nowhere in life. I never envisioned living paycheck to paycheck, but that's exactly what I was doing.

11
YOU DESERVE NOTHING

Me, Myself and Mine

Entitlement is one of the most pervasive sicknesses we have as a society. We believe that since we've achieved a certain level of education, we're entitled to a job and the success that comes with it. We're entitled to a better existence filled with life, liberty and happiness as American citizens. We're entitled to glory, fame, likes and followers. We're narcissistic success junkies. We're entitled. What we don't realize is that we deserve nothing.

Many employees assume that the company they work for has the obligation to provide special benefits for them. These benefits include 401k options, pensions, extra vacation days and other benefits that are not required by law. They fail to realize that a business' main priority is not to provide jobs, but to serve the entrepreneur. If an entrepreneur understands the necessity of having a team, they'll hire great employees. Employees don't realize that the business is actually allowing them to fill the position; unfortunately, they are dispensable. Entrepreneurs know that they aren't entitled to success just because they worked hard; success is created.

Some employees think they should be rewarded for tasks they are expected to do. They think recognition should be given to them because they are on time or early for work. They think that the company should recognize their sacrifice to perform their job related responsibilities. Recognition, rewards, and pay increases are at the discretion of the employer. Employers aren't obligated to give awards.

Businesses are not created to hold your hand or praise you. They are not your parents. They pay you to do your job (and to do it well). Do not expect your employer to look after you; it's not their job. Your future is your responsibility, no one else's. Entrepreneurs know that they can't rely on anyone else to bring them success. They know that they don't deserve anything unless they take the initiative to produce their desired outcome. No person is an island – you need teammates; however, this is not a license or carte blanche to piggyback off of another's success with the expectation of being prosperous. Nobody likes a freeloader, a leech, a moocher, a person that gives nothing but wants everything because they think they deserve it. In fact, if you rely on someone else for your success, then you'd be almost obligated to give him or her everything you receive from his or her hard work. There are also no "get rich quick" schemes, or "corner cutting" ways that lead to prosperity.

Entrepreneurs know that it takes time to build a credible brand. It takes a lot more than a good name and a catchy slogan to create a brand. You can also have the most fantastic and greatest product/service in the world, and not make a dime. It takes skills, diligence, and persistence to create a brand that will last more than five years. It also takes a lot of effort to maintain a successful business; once an entrepreneur becomes complacent they become stagnant. Once a business becomes stagnant, it leaves the door open for other entrepreneurs and businesses to take market share. Ultimately, stagnation leads to decline.

I believed, "if you build it, they will come" – "they" being customers and "it" being my website: dfta.co. However, the saying for business should be, "If you build it, market it, and distribute it correctly, they will come." Great products aren't always successful but great marketing and branding usually is.

The Trifecta of Success

Bryan Franklin, an incredibly successful college dropout turned consultant who generated $10 million from his services, believes that success is a skill that can be learned and developed. He lists the three components to success as marketing, selling, and leadership. Develop these skills and you can develop success.

As I mentioned earlier, marketing is the process of creating and keeping customers. Without this process, you can't build success. Frank Kern, a college dropout turned successful marketing consultant, preaches, "Nothing happens until something gets sold." Without sales, the business generates no income. What many people don't realize is that these skills are transferable to any and every aspect of life, yet colleges do not have required selling or leadership development courses.

We can substitute the word "customers" in our definition of marketing for "friends", "employees", or "mentors" and the skills needed are the same. The approach is the only thing that changes in the marketing process. Many people feel that marketing is synonymous with manipulating or tricking others for profit. This is likely because they've encountered cheap marketing tactics that are designed for that purpose. Instead, effective and tasteful marketing fills a need. It's a perfect pairing between a great product/service and a customer that needs it because it solves a problem. It joins individuals with similar interests that become best friends or lifelong partners. It links a job seeker with a business that needs their expertise. Marketing is the glue to society and to your success.

If you have the vision, you need as many people as possible to accept or buy into it. If you want people to respect you, they need to buy into your character. If you want people to help you, they need to buy into the reasons you give them. Therefore, nothing happens until something gets sold. When we think of selling, we think of a used car salesman in a plaid suit trying to sell us a beat up Honda. Yet, whether we realize it or not, we are constantly selling our ideals, thoughts, and character to everyone around us. If we weren't constantly selling and convincing people to help us achieve our goals, our society would not advance. You shouldn't be afraid of selling; you're a salesman. Selling is an essential skill that must be developed for success, and as an entrepreneur it is literally your bread and butter.

Leadership is not controlling people and manipulating them. Instead, a successful leader is able to stimulate and influence others to give their best efforts for the betterment of the group, organization or company as a whole. Influence isn't about tricking people. It's about commanding so much respect that people voluntarily do the things you ask of them. Leaders must have vision, and must be able to communicate that vision effectively so others will follow. They must be innovative. Effective leaders lead by example with integrity. They take responsibility for their actions.

It's the Economy, Stupid

I strongly believe economics is the most important concept that can be studied in order to figure out how the world works. Entrepreneurs must understand the basic principles of economics. We won't go too deep into the concepts and practices; I'll try to make this as painless as possible. Economics is the study of the allocation of scarce resources that have alternative uses. In English? Economics studies how efficiently a company/government/person is using the resources that they have. It studies what resources are being used, how they are being used, how effectively they are being used, and what other options those resources and tools could be used for. If you're a business owner, a basic understanding of economics can go a long way.

Earlier, I mentioned that cash flow is the lifeblood for a business. Cash is a scarce resource that can be used in many different ways. You can use cash to buy raw materials or inventory for your business to create products and sell. You can use cash to pay off debt, or pay employees. Depending on your sales and current cash position, you can make decisions that determine the future of your business. So understanding this basic principle of economics can greatly increase your chances of making your business profitable.

Your personal finances are very similar to your business. You can allocate your paycheck (your main resource) to many different uses (saving, investing or spending). Saving is what makes investment possible. Investments can be made into your business as well as other income producing assets like stocks, bonds, and real estate. A good understanding of your current economic realities (how you've been using your income to generate wealth) will help you gauge how you should allocate your future income. You should use your income to buy assets that would help you generate more income to cover your expenses and accumulate more assets. Below is a short list of income sources, liabilities and assets.

Income sources	Liabilities/Expenses	Assets
Job/Career	Rent/Mortgage	Equity
Dividends	Student Loans	Businesses
Business profits	Credit Card Debt	Stocks
Rental Income	Car/Transportation	Bonds
Freelancing	Food/Living Expenses	Real Estate
Fixed Income		
Interest		

Economics also studies supply and demand, competition and prices. If you are about to enter a crowded market (one with a lot of similar businesses/supply i.e. the Job Market) then you have to figure out a way to differentiate yourself and create demand for your product. If there is no demand for your product, you won't have customers. So you have to make sure you develop a product people want to use or a service people need. You also have to price your product or service at a price where you can cover your own expenses, make a profit, and compete with similar businesses in your niche. By having a basic understanding of economics, you will be able to manage your business a little better.

Let's say you're about to make a decision on a new product/service to offer. You will have to take into account the cost of producing this new item, how you are going to market it, what your inventory will look like after it is produced, and at what price people will be willing to pay for it. By understanding marginal revenue, marginal cost, the potential demand for what you're offering (with a little research on your competition) you should be able to gauge whether or not you should approve producing a new product, or go back to the drawing board. If you haven't already, you should buy an economics textbook, and focus on understanding microeconomic concepts since those will be the most applicable concepts for your business.

12
I'M A BIG KID NOW!

You may be looking at the sections on economics, marketing and finance and say that colleges teach these subjects. You're absolutely right! But they teach them as abstract disciplines, not to solve real world problems or the problems you would encounter while running your business. The subjects aren't made practical. They are content-oriented theory. They feed you facts that may not be relevant to you. This is pedagogical teaching, or teaching of children. You can't afford to be taught as a child if you're paying thousands of dollars and going into debt for this education. I wouldn't want to be treated as a child while trying to learn subjects that will influence the rest of my life. The solution is andragogical teaching, or teaching of adults, developed by Malcolm Knowles.

Unlike children, adults need to understand the reason for learning a concept. They need be responsible for their education. They should be guiding their learning and should have internal motivation to learn rather than motivation from someone else. Adults are more interested in learning things that are relevant to them. Adult learning is problem-centered, rather than pedagogical content-oriented learning, and experience should be its foundation. Entrepreneurs are problem solvers; it's about time you acted like an adult.

Rewarding Risk

I'm quite sure that you've heard the phrase, "without risk, there is no reward" at least once in your life. This phrase holds true for many reasons. First, it takes an effort to get out of your comfort zone. No one gets rewarded for mediocrity. The average Joe is just that: average. No one should be recognized for doing something unless it's extraordinary. Risks are exciting. They're a step into the unknown, and if the unknown yields positive results, then the person taking the risk should be rewarded. Rewards are only granted to those bold enough to take the risk required. They made the effort to break free of their comfort zone and to do something with an unknown outcome; something most people would be afraid to do. Of course, risks can have negative outcomes; otherwise they would always be guaranteed rewards.

According to this statement, we should never be rewarded unless we take a risk. I mentioned earlier that almost everything we do involves some type of risk. But each action varies as far as the probability of having a positive or negative outcome. Some tasks, like running, can vary in how negatively risky they can be. I believe risks can be both positive and negative, even simultaneously both but, typically "risk" has a negative connotation. But let's get back to the example of running. If you aren't wearing the proper footwear, or are past a certain age, running can be a dangerous risk. However, running can bring about many positive effects on your life if you take the right precautions beforehand.

The probability of experiencing a negative outcome is greatly diminished if you take the steps required to increase the chances of experiencing a positive outcome, or reward. It would be very unwise for an Olympic caliber athlete to quit running because of the slight possibility of twisting an ankle. No one rewards a coward. Avoiding the negative outcomes and increasing the likelihood of experiencing rewards is crucial for an entrepreneur, since an entrepreneur's life is filled with risks. Risks can be looked at as opportunities. Different risks yield different positive or negative opportunities. Depending on how the opportunities are used, success or failure are the results. To increase the chances of taking risks that yield positive opportunities, you have to study and prepare for the risk, so you know what actions are needed to be done. If you take on the risk of starting a business, you must do everything possible to increase the probability of your success. You have to study how to run an effective and efficient business from people who have effective and efficient businesses.

Then you have to begin the actions necessary to create your business. If you make mistakes, learn from them, but never stop taking actions to improve yourself and your business. Risks are inherent to life, so don't be afraid of them. If you're afraid of starting your business or if you're unsure if you should wait until you finish college, the best thing you can do is start now. You like to be rewarded, right?

13
THE LIST

Earlier I stated that it takes a lot of hard work to become a successful entrepreneur, but it is not impossible. If you don't believe me, here's a list constructed by YoungEntrepreneur.com of their picks for the Top 100 Entrepreneurs who succeeded without a college degree. I think it's important to note that success is defined in many ways. Success isn't only defined as monetary success, otherwise we'll only pursue money rather than meaningful and beneficial work. You may not have the same monetary success as those listed below, but be encouraged. You're self worth isn't determined by your net worth. The reward of success is in the journey, not the destination. In the next chapter I'll explain where I believe the future of education is headed.

The List

Abraham Lincoln, lawyer, U.S. president. Finished one year of formal schooling; self-taught in trigonometry, and read Blackstone on his own to become a lawyer.

Amadeo Peter Giannini, multimillionaire founder of Bank of America. Dropped out of high school.

Andrew Carnegie, industrialist and philanthropist, and one of the first mega-billionaires in the US. Elementary school dropout.

Andrew Jackson, U.S. president, general, attorney, judge, congressman. Home-schooled. Became a practicing attorney by the age of 35 - without a formal education.

Andrew Perlman, co-founder of GreatPoint. Dropped out of Washington University to start Cignal Global Communications, an Internet communications company, when he was only 19.

Anne Beiler, multimillionaire co-founder of Auntie Anne's Pretzels. Dropped out of high school.

Ansel Adams, world-famous photographer. Dropped

out of high school.

Ashley Qualls, founder of Whateverlife.com, left high school at the age of 15 to devote herself to building her website business. She was worth more than a million dollars by 17.

Barbara Lynch, chef, owner of a group of restaurants, worth over $10 million, in Boston. Dropped out of high school.

Barry Diller, billionaire, Hollywood mogul, Internet maven, founder of Fox Broadcasting Company, chairman of IAC/InterActive Corp (owner of Ask.com), dropped out of UCLA after one semester.

Ben Kaufman, 21-year-old serial entrepreneur, founder of Kluster. Dropped out of college in his freshman year.

Benjamin Franklin, inventor, scientist, author, entrepreneur. Primarily home-schooled.

Billy Joe (Red) McCombs, billionaire, founder of Clear Channelmedia, real estate investor. Dropped out of law school to sell cars in 1950.

Bob Proctor, motivational speaker, bestselling author, and co-founder of Life Success Publishing. Attended two months of high school.

Bram Cohen, BitTorrent developer. Attended State University of New York at Buffalo for a year.

Carl Lindner, billionaire investor, founder of United Dairy Farmers. Dropped out of high school at the age of 14.

Charles Culpeper, owner and CEO of Coca Cola. Dropped out of high school.

Christopher Columbus, explorer, discoverer of new lands. Primarily home-schooled.

Coco Chanel, founder of fashion brand Chanel. A perfume bearing her name, Chanel No. 5 kept her name famous. Never attended college.

Colonel Harlan Sanders, founder of Kentucky Fried Chicken (KFC). Dropped out of elementary school, later earned law degree by correspondence.

Craig McCaw, billionaire founder of McCaw Cellular. Did not complete college.

Dave Thomas, billionaire founder of Wendy's. Dropped out of high school at 15.

David Geffen, billionaire founder of Geffen Records and co-founder of DreamWorks. Dropped out of college after freshman year.

David Green, billionaire founder of Hobby Lobby. Started the Hobby Lobby chain with only $600. High school graduate.

David Karp, founder of Tumblr. Dropped out of school at 15, then homeschooled. Did not attend college.

David Neeleman, founder of JetBlue airlines. Dropped out of college after three years.

David Ogilvy, advertising executive and copywriter. Was expelled from Oxford University at the age of 20.

David Oreck, multimillionaire founder of The Oreck Corporation. Quit college to enlist in the Army Air Corps.

Debbi Fields, founder of Mrs. Fields Chocolate Chippery. Later renamed, franchised, then sold Mrs. Field's Cookies. Attended community college but never graduated.

DeWitt Wallace, founder and publisher of Reader's Digest. Dropped out of college after one year. Went back, then dropped out again after the second year.

Dov Charney, founder of American Apparel. Started the company in high school, and never attended college.

Dustin Moskovitz, multi-millionaire co-founder of Facebook. Harvard dropout.

Frank Lloyd Wright, the most influential architect of the twentieth century. Never attended high school.

Frederick "Freddy" Laker, billionaire airline entrepreneur. High school dropout.

Frederick Henry Royce, auto designer, multimillionaire co-founder of Rolls-Royce. Dropped out of elementary school.

George Eastman, multimillionaire inventor, Kodak founder. Dropped out of high school.

George Naddaff, founder of UFood Grill and Boston

Chicken. Did not attend college.

Gurbaksh Chahal, multimillionaire founder of BlueLithium and Click Again. Dropped out of H.S. at 16, when he founded Click Again.

H. Wayne Huizenga, founder of WMX Garbage Company, and helped build Blockbuster video chain. Joined the Army out of high school, and later went to college only to drop out during his first year.

Henry Ford, billionaire founder of Ford Motor Company. Did not attend college.

Henry J. Kaiser, multimillionaire & founder of Kaiser Aluminum. Dropped out of high school.

Hyman Golden, co-founder of Snapple. Dropped out of high school.

Ingvar Kamprad, founder of IKEA, one of the richest people in the world, dyslexic. Never attended college.

Isaac Merrit Singer, sewing machine inventor, founder of Singer. Elementary school dropout.

Jack Crawford Taylor, founder of Enterprise Rent-a-Car. Dropped out of college to become a WWII fighter pilot in the Navy.

Jake Nickell, co-founder and CEO of Threadless.com. Did not graduate from college.

James Cameron, Oscar-winning director, screenwriter, and producer. Dropped out of college.

Jay Van Andel, billionaire co-founder of Amway. Never attended college.

Jeffrey Kalmikoff, co-founder and chief creative officer of Threadless.com. Did not graduate from college.

Jerry Yang, co-founder of Yahoo! Dropped out of PhD program.

Jimmy Dean, multimillionaire founder of Jimmy Dean Foods. Dropped out of high school at 16.

John D. Rockefeller Sr., billionaire founder of Standard Oil. Dropped out of high school just two months before graduating, though later took some courses at a local business school.

John Mackey, founder of Whole Foods. Enrolled and dropped out of college six times.

John Paul DeJoria, billionaire co-founder of John Paul Mitchell Systems, founder of Patron Spirits tequilla. Joined the Navy after high school.

Joyce C. Hall, founder of Hallmark. Started selling greeting cards at the age of 18. Did not attend college.

Kemmons Wilson, multimillionaire, founder of Holiday Inn. High school dropout.

Kenneth Hendricks, billionaire founder of ABC Supply. High school dropout.

Kenny Johnson, founder of Dial-A-Waiter restaurant delivery. College dropout.

Kevin Rose, founder of Digg.com. Dropped out of college during his second year.

Kirk Kerkorian, billionaire investor, owner of Mandalay Bay and Mirage Resorts, and MGM movie studio. Dropped out of eighth-grade.

Larry Ellison, billionaire co-founder of Oracle software company. Dropped out of two different colleges.

Leandro Rizzuto, billionaire founder of Conair. Dropped out of college. Started Conair with $100 and a hot-air hair roller invention.

Leslie Wexner, billionaire founder of Limited Brands. Dropped out of law school. Started Limited Brands with $5,000.

Marc Rich, commodities investor, billionaire. Founder of Marc Rich & Co. Did not finish college.

Marcus Loew, multimillionaire founder of Loews theaters, co-founder of MGM movie studio. Elementary school dropout.

Mark Ecko, founder of Mark Ecko Enterprises. Dropped out of college.

Mary Kay Ash, founder of Mary Kay Inc. Did not attend college.

Michael Dell, billionaire founder of Dell Computers,

which started out of his college dorm room. Dropped out of college.

Michael Rubin, founder of Global Sports. Dropped out of college in his first year.

Micky Jagtiani, billionaire retailer. Dropped out of accounting school.

Milton Hershey, founder of Hershey's Milk Chocolate. Had a 4th grade education.

Pete Cashmore, founded Mashable.com at the age of 19.

Philip Green, Topshop billionaire retail mogul. Dropped out of high school.

Rachael Ray, Food Network cooking show star, food industry entrepreneur, with no formal culinary arts training. Never attended college.

Ray Kroc, founder of McDonald's. Dropped out of high school.

Richard Branson, billionaire founder of Virgin Records, Virgin Atlantic Airways, Virgin Mobile, and more. Dropped out of high school at 16.

Richard DeVos, co-founder of Amway. Served in the Army and did not attend college.

Richard Schulze, Best Buy founder. Did not attend college.

Rob Kalin, founder of Etsy. Flunked out of high school, enrolled in art school for a time, and faked a student ID at MIT so he could take classes. His professors subsequently helped him get into NYU because they were so impressed.

Ron Popeil, multimillionaire founder of Ronco, inventor, producer, infomercial star. Did not finish college.

Rush Limbaugh, multi-millionaire media mogul, and radio talk show host. Dropped out of college.

Russell Simmons, co-founder of Def Jam records, founder of Russell Simmons Music Group, Phat Farm fashions, bestselling author. Did not finish college.

S. Daniel Abraham, billionaire founder of Slim-Fast.

Did not attend college.

Sean John Combs, entertainer, producer, fashion designer, and entrepreneur. Never finished college.

Shawn Fanning, developer of Napster. Dropped out of college at the age of 19.

Simon Cowell, TV producer, music judge, American Idol, The X Factor, and Britain's Got Talent. High school dropout.

14
THE FUTURE OF EDUCATION

One of the last industries to be disrupted by innovation is the education industry. The Internet has played a huge part in changing the way we consume information, and it's also changed the way that people attend colleges. Online universities and online educational platforms have been growing in popularity. As more and more accredited universities begin offering online degrees, it will not only hurt the for-profit colleges that have taken advantage of young people, it will also change the way we view The College Degree. Online education (including online degrees, information websites, online academies, and iTunes U) will be to universities the way Amazon is to retail stores. Amazon hasn't displaced brick and mortar stores, but it has changed the way we shop. In the same way, the online education platforms being created today will not destroy colleges and universities as we know them, but they will have many rethinking the pursuit of a College Degree.

The stigma behind online degrees and online education programs has been fading. YouTube has become a great resource if you're trying to learn something at your own pace. As tuition continues to rise, many people will begin looking at creative ways to find the information they need for the skills they want to develop.

Here's a list of some online education platforms that are disrupting the way we view education:

Khan Academy
iTunesU
SkillShare
Udemy
YouTube

These platforms are also allowing people to earn an income by producing quality content for students. This changes the career opportunities we've grown accustomed to. Now, using platforms like Skillshare and Udemy, you can get paid to teach skills that aren't normally found in the classroom. Again, this doesn't undermine the value of teachers, but it does allow experts in diverse fields to share valuable information. This changes how we interact with field experts. It also allows people with unique skillsets to have more options in generating income. It allows people like you and me share valuable information we otherwise wouldn't be able to share.

The Future is about Value

It's always about the value you add. If you add value to your firm, you're seen as an asset. If your freelancing skills add value to me, I'll hire you. If your business products add value, I'll buy your product. If your online video or class adds value to me, I'll watch it. Value is the determining factor in each of these scenarios. It isn't about the degree or credentials you claim, it's about the actual skills and value you bring to the table. Consider what brings value to others. Consider the things you value. Consider the value of the College Degree.

In 2015, The U.S. Department of education released the College Scorecard. It's an incredible tool that allows students and parents to evaluate colleges based on their degree programs, size, average annual cost, graduation rates, and average salary after attending. I think this tool will force parents and students to consider whether or not the College Degree would add value to their life goals. It is interesting to note that the data uses the salary of students and alumni (who have received federal aid) a decade after they've enrolled. After ten years, the national average salary of those who have enrolled in a degree program is a paltry $34,300. There are better ways to create value and income for yourself than to attend college for a better living; just reread chapters 4 and 10.

Creating value is about doing the difficult (and different) things most people are afraid of doing. Creating value is about being innovative. In the Information Age, those who create and market quality content will be successful. Online education platforms are creating tremendous value for their students. Learning has become "On-Demand", where we can pause, rewind, and understand lessons on our own terms. <u>This is dramatically different from the way past generations have consumed information</u>. At the click of a mouse you can learn about logo design, then pause and restart the lesson on business development you were watching two days earlier. You're a Google search away from learning directly from an expert in your field, no application required.

The reason why these platforms add value – and while they'll revolutionize the education industry – is these platforms allow us to do things the current education system doesn't encourage. Online education platforms <u>enable us to pursue our dreams</u>. They allow us to work on what we're truly passionate about **when we want to work on them.** The future of education won't be about teaching people to comply with social norms in order to find comfort and stability in the workplace. The future of education will be about unlocking your potential. It will be about challenging our perceptions in order to find better solutions. The future is about dreaming big, and having enough courage to pursue those dreams and passions.

Sal Khan, founder of Khan Academy, had this to say about the future of education in an interview on Bloomberg:

How can we bring that spirit of entrepreneurship? How do we bring that spirit of failure not being stigmatized in the schools? The transcript of the future doesn't just have to be your GPA and your test scores. It can be your portfolio of creative works and peer feedback. Show us what you've done...We're living in a world where a smaller and smaller percentage of people are going to be able to participate in this innovation and wealth creation. We lose some of our most creative engineers and mathematicians based on how we evaluate them in middle school. We look at a twelve year old and say, "you can't mix paint, and we don't think you can be a painter. You're not flexible enough at 12 to be a dancer"...When you decouple the credential from the learning it allows everyone to compete on the learning side; it allows a lot of innovation to happen.

The future is about the crazy innovators who dream big. It's about the square pegs in the round holes that are daring enough to pursue their passion. The future is about the value creators who are troublemakers – misfits that are disrupting industry and challenging the status quo. The future is about the world changers who broke the rules we felt comfortable in. The future is for the entrepreneur.

#CollegeIsOverrated

ABOUT THE AUTHOR

Michael Hamlett, Jr. is the Founder and CEO of the lifestyle brand Don't Feed The Animals. Michael was a freshman at New York University when he decided to leverage his business knowledge to create his brand and bring value to his customers. His purpose is to challenge people's perceptions in order to find better solutions. He is adamant about educational reform, and loves to help entrepreneurs become successful business owners. He is also a Financial Coach, helping people steward their finances and learn how to build wealth. He loves to discuss finance and business on his blog:
thelionsshares.com

Connect with Me Online:
Don't Feed The Animals: **dfta.co**
Twitter: **twitter.com/dftaclothing**
Facebook: **facebook.com/dftaclothing**
Instagram: @Dontfeedtheanimals_DFTA
My blog: **thelionsshares.com**

www.ingramcontent.com/pod-product-compliance
Lightning Source LLC
Chambersburg PA
CBHW020925180526
45163CB00007B/2889

9 7 8 1 5 0 2 8 9 9 9 4 1